eBook Secrets [EXPOSED]

How to Make MASSIVE AMOUNTS OF MONEY In Record Time With Your Own eBook

Jim Edwards & David Garfinkel

eBook Secrets EXPOSED

© 2006 Jim Edwards and David Garfinkel. All rights reserved.

No part of this publication may be reproduced or transmitted in any form or by any means, mechanical or electronic, including photocopying and recording, or by any information storage and retrieval system, without permission in writing from author or publisher (except by a reviewer, who may quote brief passages and/or show brief video clips in a review).

ISBN: 1-933596-21-X (Hardcover)

Published by:
MORGAN · JAMES
THE ENTREPRENEURIAL PUBLISHER
Morgan James Publishing, LLC
1225 Franklin Ave Ste 325
Garden City, NY 11530-1693
Toll Free 800-485-4943
www.MorganJamesPublishing.com

Habitat for Humanity®
Peninsula
Building Partner

Cover and Interior Design by:
Heather Kirk
www.GraphicsByHeather.com
www.AskHeatherKirk.com
Heather@GraphicsByHeather.com

Limits of Liability / Disclaimer of Warranty:

The authors and publisher of this book and the accompanying materials have used their best efforts in preparing this program. The authors and publisher make no representation or warranties with respect to the accuracy, applicability, fitness, or completeness of the contents of this program. They disclaim any warranties (expressed or implied), merchantability, or fitness for any particular purpose. The authors and publisher shall in no event be held liable for any loss or other damages, including but not limited to special, incidental, consequential, or other damages. As always, the advice of a competent legal, tax, accounting or other professional should be sought. The authors and publisher do not warrant the performance, effectiveness or applicability of any sites listed in this book. All links are for information purposes only and are not warranted for content, accuracy or any other implied or explicit purpose.

This manual contains material protected under International and Federal Copyright Laws and Treaties. Any unauthorized reprint or use of this material is prohibited.

Special Message to the Reader

What you are about to read turns cherished notions upside down. Publishing as an industry may be the last holdout against customer-driven marketing — finding out what people want and giving it to them.

If you've ever wondered why there are so many starving writers and struggling publishing companies, that's a big part of the reason.

eBook Secrets Exposed takes a refreshingly different course. Its premise (though rarely used) is that when you produce an ebook based on what the marketplace tells you — through its actions — that it wants, then you will have a successful business venture.

A small band of Internet publishers — most of them one or two-person operations — focused on market-driven topics are making as much as $40,000 in a single month, with little or no overhead expenses other than normal Web site maintenance and the costs of processing customer payments. For you, the profit potential in this field is huge, growing and virtually unlimited.

There's never been a book before that lays out the exact methods to create an ebook that will sell and then sell it. Fortunately, both authors have ample experience in this arena. Furthermore, both are skilled and experienced teachers of practical skills. The benefit to you is they make what was once considered impossible, relatively straightforward and easy to do.

Welcome to the world of profitable e-publishing and successful authorship. And thank you for your purchase.

THE PUBLISHER

Table of Contents

Special Message to the Reader iii

Table of Contents v

You can Make Money with this eBook! vii

About the Authors ix

    Jim Edwards ix

    David Garfinkel xi

A Note from David Garfinkel xiii

Introduction by Jim Edwards xv

The Ultimate eBook Success Formula 1

    A 5-Step formula that virtually guarantees a best seller! 3

Section 1 — Making Money With eBooks 13

Section 2 — The Secret of Fast Cash 53

Section 3 — How to Build Your Own List 61

Section 4 — How to Price Your eBook for Maximum Profit 69

Section 5 — How to Make More Money With Your eBook 77

Section 6 — Heading Off Potential Problems .89

Section 7 — The Heart-Breaking Mistake Most Authors Make 95

Section 8 — 9 Ways to Create or Find a Best Selling eBook
You Can Sell for Massive Profits 105

Section 9 — How Can I Use an eBook To Get More Consulting or Coaching Business 129

Section 10 — How Do I Know My eBook Will Be a Best-Seller? 137

Section 11 — Publishing Your eBook For The Web 151

Section 12 — How to Set Up an "Auto-Pilot" eBook Delivery System . . .163

    Purchase Autoresponder Setup 169

    Mini-Course Autoresponder Setup 174

    Basics of a "Killer" Sales Letter 178

Section 13 — How To Keep People From Ripping Off Your eBook 183

Section 14 — A Surefire Way to Increase eBook Sales by Helping Your Affiliates Make More Money 197

Section 15 — "WAR Stories" 205

    Story #1 — How a 1 Hour and 20 Minute Phone Call Changed My Life! 207

    Story #2 — How I Dropped 39 Pages From My Website and Sales Went UP over 400% — Literally Overnight! 211

    Story #3 — How I can Turn Out eBooks / FREE Reports and other Large Publications VERY Quickly 213

    Story #4 — The Power of Personal Referrals Online 215

Section 16 — My Secret Method For Slashing Your Return Rate 217

Section 17 — 5 Streams of Passive Income 231

Conclusion — Where Do You Go From Here? 235

You Can MAKE MONEY With This eBook!

FACT: Nobody sells an ebook better than someone who already owns it!

You know the strong selling points of the book and can endorse it without hesitation.

You can earn generous 50% commissions just by recommending the book to people! **If you have a website, an ezine or a customer list** that would benefit from reading **"eBook Secrets Exposed"** — let them know about it!

We'll pay you 50% for every sale you make and **our affiliate program pays out twice a month**!

For Tips, Tricks and Tools for selling tons of this and other best selling ebooks, log on to:

> http://www.eBookSecretsExposed.com/affiliateinfo.shtml

Find out how you can make generous commissions (50%!) just by mentioning how happy you are with this ebook. We supply you with headlines, email teasers, pop-up scripts, graphic tools and more!

Everything you need to quickly and efficiently promote for BIG profits on every sale.

> http://www.eBookSecretsExposed.com/affiliateinfo.shtml

About the Authors

JIM EDWARDS

Jim Edwards is a dynamic and entertaining speaker who has developed, marketed and operated outrageously profitable online businesses for both himself and his clients worldwide since 1997.

Jim writes http://www.TheNetReporter.com, **a syndicated newspaper column** helping "non-technical" people use the Internet for both fun and massive profits!

Jim is a frequent guest speaker nationally at conferences and seminars on such subjects as search engine and directory traffic generation, "shoestring online marketing" and more.

He is the author and co-creator of numerous highly successful ebooks and "info-products", including:

The Lazy Man's Guide to Online Business

How to Work Less... get Paid More... and have tons more Fun! Learn the Super "Lazy Achiever" Mindset!

http://www.eBookSecretsExposed.com/lazyguide.html

How to Write and Publish your own eBook... in as little as 7 Days

"... even if you can't write, can't type and failed high school English class!"

http://www.eBookSecretsExposed.com/7dayebook.html

33 Days to Online Profits

"Finally, the First Practical, Step-By-Step, Roadmap for Internet Success No Matter What Product or Service You Sell... 100% Guaranteed!"

http://www.eBookSecretsExposed.com/33days.html

Selling Your Home Alone

http://www.eBookSecretsExposed.com/fsbo.html

The TEN Dirty Little Secrets of Mortgage Financing

http://www.eBookSecretsExposed.com/mortgagetips.html

Jim lives in Williamsburg, Virginia with his wife, daughter and four dogs. He enjoys writing, walking, softball, playing video games and listening to Frank Sinatra and Willie Nelson.

DAVID GARFINKEL

Copywriter David Garfinkel creates sales messages that deliver massive response and generate record profits. Companies and individuals working with David have made millions of dollars from his Websites, email messages, ads and sales letters.

Before he became a copywriter, David was an award-winning business journalist. David is former San Francisco Bureau Chief for McGraw-Hill World News. More recently, he was Editor-in-Chief of **What's Working Online**, a privately circulated Internet marketing newsletter subscribers paid $497 a year for.

David has been published or quoted in dozens of publications, including **bCentral, The Wall Street Journal, USA Today, Sales & Marketing Management**, and **Fast Company**. If you would like world-class assistance in revving up the selling power of **your** marketing copy, contact David by email:

David@eBookSecretsExposed.com

David's online books and courses include:

- ***Advertising Headlines that Make you Rich!***

    David has been described as "the world's greatest copywriting coach." He's a successful results oriented copywriter and his new ebook shows you exactly how to instantly adapt proven money-making headlines to your business.

    http://www.eBookSecretsExposed.com/adheadlines.html

- ***Killer Copy Tactics***

    A fully interactive multimedia course by the man many call "The World's Greatest Copywriting Coach." David will show you "how to turn words into cash" in this groundbreaking tour-de-force. This course sets the bar for what Internet based learning should be.

http://www.eBookSecretsExposed.com/killercopy.html

- **Find the Hidden Gold Mine In Your Business!**

    Money-making secrets. Includes a high-yield, low-cost action plan, packed with insider tips and techniques, to generate higher profits and make any business owner much richer in 90 days... or sooner!

    http://www.eBookSecretsExposed.com/hiddengoldmine.html

A Note from David Garfinkel

Prepare yourself for some startling information... When I sat down to interview Jim Edwards, I expected to hear some good things — but nothing like this.

What he told me, and what you're about to read, is pure "business gold." Not garden variety stuff like how to code HTML or how to write a well-structured paragraph. You can buy a book at Border's or Barnes and Noble on that, or hire people for $10 or $20 an hour to do those things. Not that they're not important things — they are.

But they're widely known. What impressed me about what's in this book is that it contains techniques and ideas that are not widely known — and that really will make you money.

I realized there is so much more to know and you can get that information from, probably, fewer than a dozen people. I know some of the other players in online publishing, and believe you me, when it comes to money-making methods, are they ever secretive. Fortunately for you, Jim Edwards is not secretive.

He is very open about what you are about to learn and after you read this ebook you will find your head spinning with surprise, shock, possibly with a bit of anger at how others may not have told you all you needed to know, and certainly with excitement about the possibilities that open up in front of you in ebook publishing.

To your outrageous success!

David Garfinkel

"The World's Greatest Copywriting Coach"

P.S. One more thing. To make it easier for you to follow along in this ebook, **my statements will be in bold** so you can determine who is speaking.

Introduction by Jim Edwards

Our purpose in this ebook, and the reason that we're doing it in interview format is so that you will feel as though I am speaking directly to *you*.

It's important to me that we're able, through this interview, to convey to you all of the secrets, all of the ideas, all of the proven tips, tricks and tactics that I have found really work and make it easier for you to sell plenty of ebooks and to make lots of money… if that's what you want to do.

What you need to remember is that there are no magic answers. There are just good, better and best ways of doing things and my objective here is to show you the best ways that I know to make massive amounts of money — in the least amount of time — with ebooks.

- How to create an ebook — whether you write it or not!
- If you don't want to create it yourself, how to find and evaluate ones you can sell
- How to sell a whole bunch of ebooks — fast!
- How to deliver them instantly and completely on autopilot
- How to collect your money with the least amount of effort as possible

Everything is presented so that, in the end, you end up with a nice stream of what we call "passive income."

So with no further ado, let's go ahead and start… and this is quite a start.

What you're about to read is **worth, conservatively, 10 times the price you paid** for this ebook! Why? Because of the strife and grief it will save you, and the money it will put in your pocket! Not 1 in 100 authors goes through this formula from start to finish… and, sadly, that's why most authors fail!

So relax and settle in for a while, because you're about to discover *The Ultimate eBook Success Formula*.

As if *eBook Secrets Exposed* isn't enough by itself, look at all these great free bonuses you get along with it!

- **BONUS #1:** Best-Selling eBook *Topic Detective*

- **BONUS #2:** Copyright Basics

- **BONUS #3:** The 'Magic' Autoresponder Message That Saves Me 1 to 3 Hours a Day in Unnecessary Emailing

- **BONUS #4:** Killer Mini Sites

- **BONUS #5:** How to Use Simple Surveys to Write Best-Selling eBooks & Info-Products

They're yours for the asking. Download them today at:

www.Morgan-James.com/ebook

Intro Section

The Ultimate eBook Success Formula

A 5-STEP FORMULA THAT VIRTUALLY GUARANTEES A BEST SELLER!

The Ultimate eBook Success Formula

A 5-STEP FORMULA THAT VIRTUALLY GUARANTEES A BEST SELLER!

DAVID: **So what's going on with ebook publishing on the Web?**

JIM: Here's the startling reality — most ebooks stink, and they are complete and total business flops!

DAVID: **Why?**

JIM: Because they're based on impulses or intuitions that the author had. Here's what I mean. Most people get what they think is a great idea for an ebook, charge off and write it — only to find that they, and maybe four other people in the world, were the only ones who wanted it!

It's a pity, because those same authors could be making a valuable contribution to other people's lives — not to mention their own bank accounts!

That's why I developed the Ultimate eBook Success Formula.

If this formula seems simple to you — it is! But quite frankly, most people don't even take this first step (let alone the other 4)....

Step 1 of the formula is to identify a niche market with a specific "high demand" need for information, preferably to satisfy either a **severe problem,** a **pressing need** or an **intense desire.**

DAVID: **Sounds great… but Jim, how do you do that?**

Jim: You don't read tea leaves or Tarot cards! You discover people's desires and problems by observing their actions. Specifically, their behavior when they are on the Internet.

You find a target audience that is ALREADY actively looking for the information you will sell online.

DAVID: **It makes sense that if they are looking for the information, then they are interested in it. That's a big "Duh!"**

How do you know they are actively searching online?

JIM: That's the beauty of this Formula. The search engines will tell you! The **Overture keyword tool** is the fastest way to find out what people are looking for.

I'll show you in step-by-step and precise detail exactly how to use this tool in great detail in **BONUS #1 — Best-Selling eBook Topic Detective**, but here's the link if you want to check it out now.

http://inventory.overture.com/d/searchinventory/suggestion/

It's really easy to use! You simply enter your keywords in this tool and see how many searches are performed each month on the Overture network.

For example, if you were writing an ebook about carpentry, then you would type in the word "carpentry." And the keyword tool will give you actual numbers, as well as related terms people search for.

Here are some sample results:

Count	Search Term
15257	carpentry
1157	carpentry school
1076	carpentry tool
838	finish carpentry
489	carpentry job
467	do it yourself carpentry
399	basic carpentry
331	carpentry project
303	carpentry tip

As you can see, carpentry has a pretty high number of searches, though it is a fairly broad topic.

But if there were only a few dozen people searching for the topic you are thinking about, then you wouldn't write a book about it.

DAVID: **That's great! It could save an author months and months of hard work on a book nobody would want!**

JIM: Exactly. You want to write an ebook that has hundreds and preferably thousands of searches for related keywords.

And here's the real tragedy. Most people don't even take this step, but for the few who do, they almost always stop here and don't take the other four steps. Big mistake!

DAVID: **What are the other four steps?**

JIM: **Step 2** is to find people who have congregated in easily identifiable places online — such as **other people's lists, ezines,**

and discussion boards. You must be able to find readily available groups of people in order to market successfully.

DAVID: **Why do you want to do this?**

JIM: To make sure you'll have an easy, direct, quick and cost-effective way to get your ebook in front of potential customers. The more people and places you can find catering to your target audience, the better! Because the places people congregate are where you can sell them your ebook.

You're looking for discussion boards, websites, ezines — publications and places that are already selling to your target audience.

The big advantage of having these Internet communities available for your marketing is that, in many cases, you won't have to put money out up front to market your ebook. You see, you can communicate quickly and cheaply with potential customers on a "per-success" basis (where you only pay sales commissions, not advertising fees) with a joint venture partner.

Use Google, Overture and Yahoo to gauge how many people and places are out there selling to your target audience.

Again, I cover how to do this in <u>great detail</u>, in Bonus 1 that comes with this book.

And, here's a warning: If you can't find enough people already selling to your target market — **don't write the book** — even if thousands of people are looking. Why? Because you'll spend all your money advertising to get sales, and there won't ever be any money left for profit!

I doubt that more than 1 in 10 or 1 in 20 authors takes these first two steps... and I only know less than a dozen people on the **entire Internet** who take these last 3 steps in order! But boy, are they reeling in the money!

DAVID: So what's step 3?

JIM: **Step 3** is to determine that **your target audience is willing to PAY for information about the topic you plan to cover in your ebook.**

Let me say that again so you don't miss it — your audience must be willing to PAY for the information you are selling!

It does you no good to find a whole lot of activity and a bunch of people and places catering to the audience that you can work with to get your sales message out there cheaply only to find out the audience won't pay for information — they only want it for free!

DAVID: **How can you tell people are willing to pay for the information?**

JIM: You look at several different factors that can tell you pretty quickly if there is money in selling to your particular audience. You look at:

- The total number of sites listed in www.yahoo.com selling to your audience.

    - Since Yahoo now charges $300 a year to list sites in the index, you can be pretty sure that if you see hundreds of sites targeting your audience that they are making some money — how much they're making, we don't know.

    - All those sites wouldn't continue spending money to advertise and keep their spot on Yahoo for that target audience if they weren't buying something.

- The quickest and best way I know is simply to go to the pay-per-click search engine www.Overture.com and search for your keywords. If you have a keyword that has tens-of thousands of searches a month, but you can buy the word for $.05 a click (the minimum bid) that's a BAD sign!

    - That means lots of people are searching, but nobody has found a way to make money with that traffic… and don't think you are going to change their minds because your ebook is "better" than all those other products.

I'll tell you a story later of how I skipped this third step (misinterpreted it) and it cost me about 2 weeks of solid work and a chunk of money too!

DAVID: **You mean you didn't just dream up this information one fine day when you had nothing better to do?**

JIM: Hardly. This knowledge comes complete with "battle" scars. That's what trial-and-error learning is all about. But what I just told you is field-tested, proven, and actually making me money right now as we're talking about it.

So if you pass the first three steps I've just given you, then you are already miles ahead of the competition. But these last 2 steps are what truly separate the super-achievers from the average online ebook sellers!

DAVID: **So what's Step 4?**

JIM: **Step 4 is: Write your sales letter first!** Before you write a word of your actual ebook (or before you have someone else do it for you), first write a sales letter to sell your ebook (on a

Web site). Make the kind of promises that will be most appealing to your market!

Create your ultimate information product in your imagination first, and don't put any limits on what goes into it, or what it can do for your customers.

Since it hasn't been created yet, there really are no limits on you for what it can be, what it can teach and the exact way it solves the problem for the reader.

DAVID: **Most people create the ebook first and then create copy to sell it. What's wrong with that?**

JIM: If you already have created the ebook then you will have "limits" on you when you write the sales copy. You're trying to make the sales letter fit the ebook — instead of making the ebook fit the "perfect" sales letter!

So when you write the copy that will go up on the Web site to sell your ebook — go crazy, go wild!

Describe exactly what the ebook will do, teach and offer for your target audience. Describe the most tantalizing, delicious, perfect ebook they could ever want, need or desire.

If you do this and really let your imagination run wild you will be so excited to create the ebook NOTHING will stand in your way of creating it!

DAVID: **OK, that makes sense. So what do you do after you write the sales letter?**

JIM: After you write the sales letter for the "perfect ebook" then simply use this sales letter as the literal blueprint for creating your ebook. Just create what you wrote up in the sales letter.

(Editor's note: You'll find information on sales letters both on page146 "Basics of a Killer Sales Letter" as well as a complete step-by-step method for writing sales letters in Bonus 4, "Killer Mini Sites.")

DAVID: **Alright. What's Step 5?**

Once you know there is an active ONLINE audience looking for information, and you have a cheap, easy and fast way to reach them, and they are willing to pay for information and you have written your ultimate sales letter as the blue print, then you're ready to move ahead.

Step 5 is to create your ebook FAST using one of the many quick and easy methods we'll teach you later in this course — even if you don't write the ebook yourself!

DAVID: **Man, that sure is different from what most authors and publishers do. I don't think traditional publishing people would even understand what you're talking about — because you're approaching this as a BUSINESS! What a refreshing, new idea.**

So can you sum up this section for us and then we'll move on?

JIM: Sure. Let me summarize the formula…

Step 1 — <u>Identify a target audience actively looking for information online</u>. It does you no good to write an ebook that a lot of people aren't already looking for information on the topic.

Step 2 — <u>Make sure there are lots of sites and people already selling to them and in communication with them on a</u>

regular basis. These will be your future joint venture partners and your fastest means of selling massive amounts of ebooks.

Step 3 — Your target audience must be willing to pay for the information you will offer. It does you no good to write an ebook if your target audience expects to get everything for free — or can easily already get the information you will sell them for free elsewhere. *(Editor's reminder: Detailed information on how to do Steps 1 through 3 in Bonus 1, "Best-Selling eBook Topic Detective.")*

Step 4 — Write the sales letter first! Create the most compelling blueprint by first creating the sales letter with no limits!

Step 5 — Create your ebook using one of the quick and easy techniques we will teach you in this ebook! (And 3 of the 11 techniques we'll show you don't even require you to write it yourself!)

DAVID: **Very good. Now, let's move on to the subject of making money...**

Section 1

Making Money With eBooks

Making Money With eBooks
SECTION 1

DAVID: **How much money can someone make, really, writing and selling ebooks on the Web?**

JIM: You mean, like $800 a month? Or $4,500 a month? Or $9,500 a month? Or is it possible to make over $20,000 a month with an ebook?

DAVID: **Yes, that is what I was wondering.**

JIM: Well, all of those things are possible. Depending on which ebook and which author, they're happening right now. They've happened for me and they've happened for others. In my ventures, we've done it with almost zero start-up money, and we didn't have any special advantages. We've made money the very first day the ebook was out.

But how much money you'll make depends more than anything else on three factors: 1) the <u>size of your audience</u>; 2) how many of them are <u>willing to pay for the information</u> that you are going to sell in ebook form; and 3) how many of those people who are willing to buy your information <u>can you put your ebook sales message in front of</u> cheaply enough so that they can buy it and you still make money.

I have some ebooks where I make a $1,000 a month, then I have others where I make between $5,000 to $10,000 a month. It really just depends on the size of the audience, how well you target them, and how much it costs you to get your sales message in front of them.

But here's the most important question I think anyone should consider when they're looking at doing an ebook:

> Would you be happy if you could take action one time by creating or finding an ebook, putting it up on the internet and then devoting only about 3 to 6 hours a week to marketing the book?
>
> Once the ebook and sales letter are done, your primary job would be getting it out there and finding new joint venture partners. <u>If you only made $250, $300 a week extra for 3 to 6 hours worth of work a week, would you be happy</u>?
>
> Would that make a difference in your life?

DAVID: **That's a great question. But let me just follow up on some of the numbers you mentioned. Is it really possible? Ok, I can believe $250 a week, but what about $10,000 a month? I mean, how many people can really do something like that?**

JIM: How many? It really depends on an individual's ingenuity and persistence. The field is wide open and growing very rapidly. There's still plenty of room and there will be for at least a couple of years to come.

Here's what's important: If you can find the right target market, a market with a major problem that they're willing to pay money to solve, or if you have a juicy enough tid-bit or collection of information that someone's willing to pay for so that they can get a desired result, then you can join the select group of people who are now making <u>more than $10,000.00 month... and some of them are even doing that a week!</u>

DAVID: **Okay, so could you explain what you mean by "finding a market?"**

JIM: Okay. Finding a market means that you're not trying to sell to everybody online. You're trying **only** to sell to a "Niche Market."

DAVID: **What's that?**

JIM: Well, there are a hundred million people on the Internet — maybe two hundred million, nobody knows for sure. Each of those people belongs to smaller sub-groups called "Niche Markets". A Niche Market is simply a group of people that share a <u>common interest</u> or a <u>common problem</u>.

What you're interested in finding is a Niche Market that has a very specific problem that you can solve or a very specific interest you can give them more highly specialized information about. Or, one that has a need or want that you can meet with the information and knowledge contained in your ebook.

DAVID: **Okay. Could you give me an example of a Niche Market that might be large enough and have a problem they would be willing to spend money for it so that I could really make some "big money"?**

JIM: Okay — here are some larger markets that have readily identifiable niche markets within them:

1. <u>Real Estate / Mortgages</u> — the largest purchase of most people's lives

2. <u>Health / Wellness</u> — as the population ages people are always looking for ways to look and feel better

3. <u>Personal Finances</u> — people are always looking for ways to maximize their personal finances

4. <u>Relationships</u> — how to improve, save or enhance your relationships with a lover, family member, your boss, co-workers

5. <u>Computers / Software</u> — people need to learn how to get the most out of their computers, software packages, hardware and anything else. This one is ever-changing as new programs come out, upgrades, etc.

6. <u>Entertainment</u> — Lots of people who go online are looking to be entertained, amused or distracted. I saw an ebook that showed you how to do levitation (they even had a demo video on their site). Apparently that guy is cleaning up selling an ebook on how to do magic tricks that will amaze your friends and make you more popular.

7. <u>Employment</u> — People regularly go online to find out about employment in certain industries, look for jobs, find interviewing tips, tips on how to interview people, recruiting and retaining good people, etc.

Those are examples of larger niche markets. But let me give you an example of even more refined "niche" markets within each of those. Let's look at Real Estate / Mortgages because I am <u>very</u> familiar with that one.

Within that niche there are:

- People looking to purchase a new construction home
- People looking to purchase a vacation home
- People looking to purchase a timeshare
- People looking to buy investment property as a tax shelter

- People looking for real estate tax help and advice
- People looking for how to get the best financing on their next home
- People looking to refinance a home to a lower rate or fewer years... or both
- People looking to finance a new home or investment property with "creative financing', 'zero down' strategies
- People looking to act as their own building contractor
- People looking to buy and rehab houses and then "flip" them for quick profits
- People looking to buy and sell discounted "seller" financing notes on real estate

Needless to say I could go on for another couple of pages! But those are examples of niche markets within larger markets where people are spending money on ebooks!

DAVID: **Wow! I'm sure you could go on for a while longer! So what would I do next?**

Once you pick your Niche Market, then you need to understand how to present or "angle" the information to get the maximum number of those people interested. You can do that using the top ten (10) reasons or motivations for people to buy anything — especially information products. Here they are:

1. The number one reason people buy anything is to <u>make money</u>.

2. The second most popular reason anyone buys anything is to <u>save money</u>.

3 Third is to save time.

4 Fourth is to avoid effort.

5 Fifth is to get more comfort.

6 Sixth is to achieve greater cleanliness.

7 Seventh is to attain fuller health.

8 Eighth is to escape physical pain.

9 Ninth is to gain praise.

10 Tenth is to be popular.

If, say, you want to make $10,000 a month, then your best bet is to find a way to show a specific target audience of people something of interest to them in one of the top four categories — how to make money, save money, save time, and/or avoid effort. In fact, if you can do all four of those in one ebook, then you should have a real winner!

DAVID: **Could you walk us through an example of how you would do this?**

JIM: Sure, let's use the "employment" category and, using the techniques in the Bonus #1 "Best-Selling eBook Topic Detective" we do a search on the Overture keyword tool for the general term "employment". Scanning down the list we see over 11,000 searches for "employment search" — this might be a great niche market within the overall employment niche.

Now let's assume you do your research and there are a lot of sites out there selling to this audience and they appear to be willing to do joint ventures. And let's also assume this audience will pay for information if they think it will help them.

In researching this audience we want to identify and list their common problems. We also want to be on the lookout for other people already selling information to this audience to see what looks like a proven seller and the problems they solve or the needs and wants they satisfy for the target audience.

Let's list off some problems people who are looking for a job almost certainly will have one or more of:

NOTE: With all of these employment problems there is usually a real sense of <u>urgency</u>. An audience with an <u>immediate</u> and <u>pressing</u> need usually makes for a great target audience.

1. They either don't have a job right now or they have a job/ boss they hate — and they need a new job fast.

2. They may know a layoff is coming and don't want to wait for the "end".

3. They are probably scared and upset about how they will pay their bills and feed their family if they go without a job for more than a couple of weeks.

4. They are concerned about losing their benefits package and health insurance.

5. They want to know what will happen to their retirement package — what options they might have.

6 They are scared of the whole interviewing process.

7 They are scared of sending out resumes and having their current boss find out they are "looking".

I'm sure there are two dozen more problems they might have but this is enough for this example. Now let me show you how you frame this into an ebook concept.

Let's take another look at the top 10 reasons people buy information and brainstorm the ways we could create an ebook that solved their problems with the angle of each of the reasons:

1 <u>make money</u> — Show them how they can find a better paying job using their same skill sets or reveal quick and easy ways to upgrade their skills and get a better job.

Possible bullet or headline — "How to finally get paid everything you're worth!"

2 <u>save money</u> — Show them how they can use the Internet to save hundreds of dollars on printing and postage over sending their resume through the mail in the "traditional" way.

Possible bullet or headline — "Save hundreds — even thousands — of dollars in postage and printing sending out resumes nobody reads anyway! We'll show you quick, easy and free ways to get your resume into the hands of employers who want to hire you!"

3 <u>save time</u> — Show them how to use websites to find the right job postings and avoid spending hours looking through the classifieds.

Possible bullet or headline — "Little-known secrets for using job posting boards like Monster.com to wade through thousands of want ads to quickly find the jobs you want… and with just a few clicks of a mouse!"

4 <u>avoid effort</u> — Show them how to use the Internet as a networking tool so they don't have to endure weeks and months of searching in vain for a new job.

Possible bullet or headline — "Learn the secrets for finding the 'good' jobs nobody advertises by harnessing the incredible networking power of the Internet. But be careful! Don't violate the three cardinal rules of online networking etiquette. Do you know what they are?"

5 <u>get more comfort</u> — This one is pretty simple. Show them how to get a better job at higher pay.

Possible bullet or headline — "Imagine yourself making $500 to $2,000 more each month just by going to a job where you are finally appreciated and valued for your contributions!"

6 <u>achieve greater cleanliness</u> — I don't think this one applies.

7 <u>attain fuller health</u> — This one might revolve around their benefits package and how to negotiate a better benefits package with a new employer, even an employer who doesn't normally provide health coverage.

Possible bullet or headline — "How to negotiate for a better health insurance plan for your family — even if a prospective employer doesn't normally provide coverage. We'll even show you how to negotiate your way out of the usual 'mandatory' waiting period."

8 <u>escape physical pain</u> — Give them several ways to relieve stress they might be feeling over their current situation.

Possible bullet or headline — "5 quick and easy ways to reduce stress and concentrate on the task at hand... finding a new job you'll love and will pay you every dime you are worth and more!"

9. <u>gain praise</u> — This could be two-fold: praise from a new boss or praise from friends and family members over how great their new job will be once they get it using the information you sell them.

Possible bullet or headline — "Imagine how proud your family will be when you come home and announce, "Our troubles are over... I just accepted a new position with a great company at a much higher rate of pay!"

10. be popular. — Refer to number 9

Once you've identified a niche market, identified their pressing problem, intense pain, or intense desire, and seen how those problems and needs correlate to the list of why people buy, the next step it to create the concept for your ebook.

In this case, based on research and knowing what is out there in the marketplace, I would think that an ebook that addressed these problems would do very well if it were crafted specifically for using specific Internet tools and techniques to help a person in their job search.

Also, if you could find a specific profession that had a lot of turnover or was experiencing turmoil, you could create a customized version(s) of the ebook or special bonus reports aimed at a specific industry.

A potential title for this ebook might be:

The Online Job Hunter "Powerful, yet little-known Internet Tips, Tricks and Tools to help you quickly and easily find a better paying job you'll love!"

So that is the actual evaluation and thought process I go through.

DAVID: **That's excellent! Can you give us an example of how you used this with one of your existing books?**

Sure! There are several people making money selling real estate related books, and real estate is one of the most researched topics online. In fact, last month there were almost a half a million searches for the phrase "real estate" on Overture.

At some time in their lives, real estate is a very important subject to most people. You've heard the old saying about your house being the biggest investment etc. Real estate, in general, is something people take very seriously and do a lot of fact-finding online… a potentially perfect environment for online ebook sales (as long as they are willing to pay for the information).

I have a real estate related book, and I have chosen to go after the niche market of "for sale by owner" sellers. These are people who want to sell their house without a real estate agent or broker. Their main motivation is to save the 6% commission most brokers charge.

I did this for several reasons:

1. <u>This is a market that is highly identifiable online</u> — I'm going after people who want to sell without an agent and who have the specific objective of saving the commission.

2. <u>There is a lot of research being done online on this topic</u> — There are over 108,000 searches a month for the phrase "for sale by owner", so I know there is activity online.

3. <u>There are a lot of sites already selling to them</u> — Surfing around the net using the techniques I teach in Bonus #1 you can see there are a lot of "for sale by

owner" sites already selling information, products and services to this audience. Potential joint venture partners seem quite plentiful.

As far as the subject, my ebook meets the top 3 of the top 4 reasons people buy information online:

First, to save money — my ebook tells them exactly how to save the 6% commission most agents charge. To some families that means saving $6,000 to $15,000 in commission. This is a powerful motivator to buy the ebook! In fact, it's so powerful it is the subject of my site's main headline.

Second, to save time — my ebook lays out all the steps they need to go through to get the house sold. It shows them how to advertise effectively, negotiate, pricing the house and more. It keeps them from making mistakes that will make their sales and marketing efforts take much longer than they should!

Third, to avoid effort — by showing them exactly what to do, they don't have to do anything more than is necessary to get the home sold and save the commission. I promise simple, powerful action steps virtually anyone can follow!

So that's a way I have used this process for creating an ebook that makes money, though when I originally did it I didn't have it nearly down to a science like I do now. I wish I could have read this book about 5 years ago!

DAVID: **No kidding! What's the name of your real estate book?**

JIM: The book is, "Selling Your Home Alone" at www.fsbohelp.com and I have been selling that online since 1997.

DAVID: **Can I ask how much you make per month?**

JIM: This one ebook consistently makes enough each month to pay my house payment, two car payments and the electric bill!

DAVID: So your monthly commission covers a lot. It sounds like it covers almost all of your living expenses except your groceries.

JIM: Oh, definitely! And it has for a while now. In fact, that book made it possible for me to get away from my job and devote myself to this full time and enjoy the results that I've achieved.

DAVID: Okay, and of course, that's one of your lowest selling books (volume), I would imagine?

JIM: That is one of the lower volume selling books, right.

DAVID: Okay.

JIM: Now, another example of ebooks that do quite well are ebooks that have to do with the purchase of "big ticket" items... especially if they can help people save money or make every dollar they do spend go even further.

There are several automobile related books that do well. [The late] Corey Rudl has one, I believe it is www.carsecrets.com that his company still sells after many years.

It shows people how to negotiate the best deal on their next new or used car, as well as dealing with car maintenance issues and things of that nature.

Even though his company is now famous for online marketing, they still makes a lot of money from that site.

Right on the site he says over 21,000 people have paid him $27 — that equals $567,000 in sales over 6 years, or an average of $94,500 in sales per year.

I'd say that qualifies as big money!

DAVID: **Yes, it does.**

JIM: But it's not just things that deal with a big purchase, it can be anything that deals with a significant life issue. I know another guy who sells an ebook on how to stop your divorce and he says <u>he is making about $35,000.00 a month</u> with that book.

DAVID: **That's impressive.**

JIM: Sure! He sells this ebook that is like 110-112 pages long. I've looked at it, its got good information in it and he sells it for $79.00. But, again, you don't want prospects thinking of what you've created as just another book. **They need to see it as more than just a book.**

HOT TIP: In order to make the big money, you've got to have them seeing the purchase of your ebook, not as the purchase of a "book", but the purchase of a <u>self-contained solution to their painful problem</u> or the way to <u>obtain an intensely desirable result</u>!

DAVID: **I see what you mean. Like a solution to not get ripped off at your car dealer or a solution on how to avoid an expensive and emotionally painful divorce.**

JIM: Right. Or, how not to pay a real estate agent a six (6%) commission that could actually represent <u>half the equity</u> that you have accumulated in your home!

As soon as you start thinking about your ebook as being a solution to a particularly tough problem that your market has, then you're well on your way to making much more money with it.

DAVID: **Okay. So, I'm starting to get the picture that it's not like you write an ebook on any topic that strikes your fancy and just post it for sale on a website. Instead, you find out what people want and are willing to pay for, and you create your ebook focused on that information. And you can make a lot of money if you've got a good product appealing to the right market.**

JIM: Correct.

DAVID: **Then let me ask you this. Say I write my ebook, how fast can I expect to make this money?**

JIM: Well, I've had ebooks where we finished writing the ebook on a Thursday and by the following Tuesday we were making money.

DAVID: **Really?!**

JIM: And we're making a whole lot of money.

DAVID: **Like how much?**

JIM: Over $42,000.00 in the first 30 days!

DAVID: **You're kidding!**

JIM: No.

DAVID: Did the sales stick? Did you get a lot of refunds?

JIM: No, we did not get a lot of refunds. Our refund rate is less than five (5%) percent.

DAVID: That's very good.

JIM: Which is better than what I hear some other people say that they get… if they'll even talk about it.

DAVID: Yeah. Can I ask which book that was?

JIM: That was the "33 Days to Online Profits" that I co-wrote with Yanik Silver.

DAVID: That's fabulous!

Now, let's say I have identified this market, sort of in the abstract, and I write the book. Who's going to buy this book now that it's written?

JIM: First of all I would encourage everyone to go back and read the "Ultimate eBook Success Formula" we just covered at the beginning of the book. I sure hope nobody who buys this course ever writes an ebook and then asks "Who is going to buy it?"

<u>You'd better know exactly who is going to buy your ebook BEFORE you write it!</u>

We're going to talk about this in-depth here in a few minutes, but the upshot is, the fastest way to find someone to buy your ebook is to find other people who are selling online who already have the ear of your target audience.

DAVID: **Okay. So you find someone who has already gathered a niche market audience and they've established a good relationship with that market and you...**

JIM: Give them a piece of the pie... but only <u>after</u> they've already sold the pie for you!

DAVID: **Give them a piece of the pie...very good. You don't pay them until after they have already made the sale!**

But the bottom line is, can anyone create and market an ebook this way?

JIM: Yes. Anyone can do this — with a couple of critical points to remember.

DAVID: **Okay.**

JIM: Number one, you've got to <u>believe</u> you can do it and you've got to <u>want</u> to do it very much.

DAVID: **Okay, and number 2?**

JIM: Number two, you have to understand that these are not magic answers, but these are proven formulas and specific action steps. Meaning, in order to make it happen, <u>you have to take action</u>. So you can't just wish it will happen, you can't just hope it will happen, but you have to take this information and act on it.

But don't worry, I'm going to show you how to create ebooks even if you can't write. I'm going to show you how to get your very own ebook that you have the rights to that you can sell.

DAVID: **We're still talking about making big money, right?**

JIM: Yes.

DAVID: **So, how do I make the maximum amount of money in the minimum amount of time with my ebook and sell a whole lot of them real fast?**

JIM: You find what is called a "joint venture" or JV partner. Remember I told you before that you want to find somebody who has the ear of your audience? What you want to do is go find people that have large lists of customers or prospects, they have people's email addresses and permission to send them email and, in this case, they would send them an email <u>strongly</u> endorsing your ebook.

DAVID: **How do I find these people?**

JIM: I'll get to that in a moment. Just remember, you should not write your ebook until you know exactly what paths you are going to use to market it and you've done the proper research on your audience's wants and needs.

I'll say right here, that's the biggest mistake virtually every ebook author makes!

DAVID: **Including the one who's asking you the questions.**

JIM: Here's what happens when you write the ebook first...

You've got a great idea for a book, you go and you spend days and weeks and months writing it, poring over it, thinking about it, creating this thing and then all of a sudden an ebook pops out the other end and you've got to go find a market for it.

DAVID: **You know...I'm just thinking about the ebooks that I have done. If I had more specifically tuned them to a niche market, I probably would have sold two to five times as many.**

JIM: And you would have written them differently and it wouldn't have been any harder to write them.

DAVID: **Actually it would have been easier because I would have been writing for a specific type of person in mind.... I would have focused exclusively on their needs rather than worrying about the "general" audience.**

JIM: Yes. And you would have been writing it specifically for the needs of your customer rather than writing it how you wanted to write it and then trying to jam the customer into your ebook, rather than providing an ebook that exactly met the needs they said they had... not the needs you <u>thought</u> they had.

DAVID: **That's ok. I'll go easy on myself. I finally had to write and sell three (3) ebooks to learn that. So...**

JIM: [Laugh]

DAVID: **Yeah...ok...**

JIM: So that's why we need to talk about the marketing first so that you can work backwards from the marketing to the writing of the ebook. Creating the actual ebook delivery is a relatively easy thing that you can either do yourself, or you can hire somebody to set up for you.

DAVID: **Well, let me get a spatula, scrape my jaw off the floor and see if I understand what you're saying.**

The first step to writing the ebook is figuring out how you're going to sell it, who you're going to sell it to and, unless you have a huge list of people in place who are already used to taking your advice on the Internet, then you probably want to go find a joint-venture partner, right?

JIM: Yes. In fact, you <u>must</u> at least identify a whole <u>group</u> of potential JV partners. You may or may not contact them ahead of time. You probably won't contact them unless you already know them or unless you have already been in contact with them before. You just want to identify them so you know there are a lot of potential people to help you sell your ebook once it's ready to sell.

HOT TIP If you can only find one or two people already selling to your target audience you need to get <u>scared</u>! Most of the time that means the audience is either not profitable, hard to reach or expensive to sell to.

DAVID: **Okay.**

JIM: Once you identify a group of potential JV partners, you need to see who they are. Who are they talking to, how many are there, what other kinds of offers do they make, what other kinds of products do they endorse, what kinds of their own products do they invent, write or push?

DAVID: **But how do you find them?**

JIM: You find them a couple of different ways. The first way is to look at yourself.

Take a hard look at the emails you get, ezines you subscribe to, the online community discussion groups you read, the regular off-line books you read, all the things that you have or receive from people <u>who have people</u> that are just like you that they communicate with regularly — preferably through email.

Look through the ezines you receive. Everybody receives ezines, those email newsletters that come to your inbox every day.

Look at the ebooks you've bought. Look at your favorite authors. Look at the people who are already talking to the audience that you're in because chances are, the ebook that you write, especially the first or second one, is going to be aimed at a target audience you're already a member of.

So, you want to identify the people you know or are familiar with that you already have communications from and look to see if they do any kind of joint-venture type deals.

All these sources go on your "A" List because you are already familiar with the quality of their work and their reputation.

DAVID: **Okay, Is there a "B" List; are there other ways to find other joint venture partners?**

JIM: Yes. In fact, looking for more and new JV partners is a never-ending process.

When you're researching your ebook topic, you're going to become very familiar with the "keywords" your target audience is interested in and so the next thing you do is start using those keywords to search Google, Yahoo and especially Overture where you know people are actually paying to get really good placement for certain keywords.

DAVID: **You mention Overture because it's a "pay-per-click" search engine, right?**

JIM: Yes, it's a pay-per-click search engine service where people pay money every single time somebody clicks on their link.

You want to do searches for the main keywords your target audience is going to use when they're looking for information. You want to look to see which sites come up consistently and then you're going to want to go to those websites and investigate them.

Look to see if they collect people's email addresses, see if they have an ezine, find out if they sell a whole bunch of products that are either competitive or complementary to yours. Don't worry about it right now if they sell something that seems competitive, because everybody owns more than one cookbook, or more than one book on writing, or more than one book on any other subject that really interests them.

DAVID: **Yeah, you're absolutely right. When you get interested in the subject, if you are an information purchaser, you may end up buying four or five books about the same subject very quickly.**

I have several topics I'm interested in, and I have twenty or thirty books, or more, about each of them. Sales and marketing and writing copy and all of those things...so maybe I'm an extreme case, but you

know, you make a real good point that a lot of authors or marketers might forget. If someone has bought one book about a topic, they will probably buy a lot more than one.

JIM: Right. And then the other thing that you do is, you start asking for referrals to potential joint venture partners.

DAVID: Oh really? How does that work?

JIM: Asking for referrals sounds like good old-fashioned sales — and it is!

This step comes later in the process. At first, you're just trying to get a feeling for the size of the market, but once you know that the market is there, and you've identified how big the market is, then you would simply send an email to a potential partner asking them if they would be interested in doing a joint-venture with you once your ebook is done and you're ready to start selling.

There is a certain way that you present your case where you tell them what your conversion is off your sales letter and things like that.

Here's an example of a letter I have used with success…

> Subject: [firstname] — New product for you to sell
>
> Dear [firstname],
>
> I found your [site name] site today through the ClickBank Marketplace and I was quite impressed with your [make a nice comment about the site].

I especially liked [make another comment about what you liked].

The reason I'm writing is to introduce an idea that could create an additional stream of income for you with no risk.

Let me explain.

My name is Jim Edwards and I'm the co-author (along with Joe Vitale — http://www.mrfire.com) of a new ebook entitled,

"How to Write and Publish your own eBook in as little as 7 Days"

This incredible resource helps ordinary people create, write and publish their own ebook in as little as *one week*.

The ebook has been endorsed by some of the web's great marketers, including:

~ Larry Chase (Web Digest for Marketers)

~ Yanik Silver (Instant Sales Letters)

~ Jay Conrad Levinson (Guerrilla Marketing)

~ David Garfinkel (Advertising Headlines)

~ many others!

*** Our sales letter is currently converting visitors at a rate of 2.3% — 6.7% depending on the focus of the traffic! ****

We've just setup an affiliate program where you earn a FULL 50% commission everytime your referrals buy.

*** That means for every 100 targeted visitors you send us you could make as much as $90 or more!

The book's unique selling proposition is quite exciting —

"How to write and publish your own OUTRAGEOUSLY Profitable eBook in as little as 7 days... even if you can't write, can't type and failed high school English class!"

It's at: http://www.7dayebook.com and if you visit, you'll see that it seems very complementary to what you offer.

In fact, here's a review copy for you to preview our ebook for yourself:

===> http://www.7dayebook.com/rvw/revw.shtml

** Please note the preview copy will only be available for the next 72 hours.

I think you'll agree this ebook could create another great source of revenue for you while providing a valuable service to your customers.

You can find out all the details at:

http://www.7dayebook.com/affiliateinfo.shtml

Or, if you'd like to discuss this with me personally you can call me anytime, 757-715-2157 or email me — mailto:info@7dayebook.com and I'll explain everything in full detail.

We look forward to working with you.

> Sincerely,
>
> Jim Edwards & Joe Vitale
>
> http://www.7dayebook.com
>
> mailto:info@7dayebook.com
>
> P.S. We've received a tremendous response, but the field is still wide open. Take advantage of this opportunity now!
>
> P.P.S. Please remember the Review copy will only be available for the next 72 hours — so act now while it's fresh in your mind.
>
> ===> http://www.7dayebook.com/rvw/revw.shtml

JIM: And then, if they turn you down, you simply ask them for a referral:

"Well that's okay, I understand, who else do you know that caters to my target audience that might be interested in talking to me about doing a joint venture?"

DAVID: Okay, so you're saying, initially, your going to identify people, but you're not going to talk to them right away?

JIM: Not yet, you want to see what they're doing, what they're selling, what they've got going on, make sure there are enough of them so you're not pinning all your hopes on what one or two people <u>might</u> do for you and…

DAVID: Okay...so it's sort of like a reconnaissance thing, like you're a spy. You're doing a little competitive intelligence here.

JIM: Right. In fact, we haven't even decided yet whether or not to write our ebook. We just want to make sure that there's a bunch of people out there to sell it for us if we do.

DAVID: Okay. So, I'm just going to take a big "hunch" leap right here and say, the worst thing you can do when you're trying to make money with an ebook is to blaze new trails. The best thing you can do is find existing markets because they're usually right to buy new ebooks, correct?

JIM: Exactly! You want to find existing trails so you can bring your ebook down that trail that somebody has already spent the time, energy and effort to cut the path.

DAVID: And...and the fear that nobody will want to buy it is probably groundless because the people who buy one will usually buy several since they'll each contain new information as well as overlapping parts that reinforce one another.

JIM: Sure, and you don't have to write on the exact same topics that everybody else is writing on, just in the same area.

DAVID: Okay, good. So, now I understand that before I start to go out to all these joint venture partners, I'm going to want to have some kind of track record. I'll have to start close to home, maybe with somebody I already know or someone who's willing

to take a risk on me, but after I've got one and a proven track record of results, I'm going to want to go out to a lot of them, right?

JIM: Right... and you want to do it <u>fast</u> and furious when you do it! Once you start rolling it out you do it as big as you can with as many people as you can.

DAVID: **And...so tell me how do I motivate them to work with me?**

JIM: Okay, a bigger joint venture partner is going to decide within a minute and a half or faster whether they are ever going to do anything with you or not.

DAVID: **Why? Why do they decide so quickly?**

JIM: Because they are busy. Because they are working on new projects themselves. They are thinking about what they're going to send out to their list next. They're working on a new ebook, they're looking for their own joint venture partners.

They're running a business, and the bigger person or organization you contact, the more they get contacted. Those people might get contacted fifteen, twenty, thirty times a week... maybe even that many times a day!

DAVID: **Really?**

JIM: Sure! They get contacted by people asking them to do stuff and they will look at things, but you've got to be able to tell them these two things: 1) You've got to tell them how much they are going to make per sale. 2) You've also got to be able to tell them how many people out of every 100 that show up to your website purchase.

DAVID: **Okay.**

JIM: And that's pretty much what you need to be able to tell them up front to get their attention. Then you need to be able to explain how your ebook would benefit their audience.

DAVID: **Is there anything you need to do to make it easier for them to promote your ebooks... even to the point they don't have to read it or write a sales letter themselves?**

JIM: Yes. You really should be able to give them what's called "proven copy". Now when you know what your conversion rate is off your website, that is called having "proven copy".

How "proven" it is or not, depends on the percentage, but if you can get between two (2%) and four (4%) percent of the people who show up to your website to buy, then you definitely have "proven copy".

The other thing you must be able to supply these people is a proven email teaser that they can adapt or use "as is" to send out to their own list.

DAVID: **What do you mean by "email teaser"?**

JIM: An email teaser is one of those emails that everybody gets that says, in effect...

MAKING MONEY WITH EBOOKS

Subject: Joe, Incredible New Resource for you

Hi Joe,

Jim Edwards here from www.fsbohelp.com (make sure they know the person sending the email). I had to tell you about this great new resource I just found, it's called

"How to Save $6,179.00 in real estate commission by selling your house yourself."

Now, based on the relationship that you and I have where you trust me to supply you with information about real estate and related issues I thought you would be very interested in finding out more about this incredible new resource.

1. It has some great benefits for you:

2. It shows you exactly how to find FREE advertising

3. It teaches you how to negotiate with nervous buyers

4. It shows you how to assemble a team of professionals to help you sell — without paying a commission

5. Sets you up to handle all the legal aspects of the sale

6. Price your home for maximum profit

7. … and all the other aspects of pricing, negotiating, closing and settling on a home.

> It was written by Jim Edwards, who has a proven track record in this business and I got him to give us a special deal for our subscribers.
>
> I urge you to go ahead and check it out now.
>
> Click here ➔ Their affiliate link

Now this is a pretty basic teaser, but it follows a proven formula.

1. Catch their attention with a compelling headline
2. Remind them of who you are
3. Introduce the resource and why you are telling them about it
4. List off the juicy bits about it
5. Tell them about the author and why they should take his or her advice
6. Drive them to action (click the link)

DAVID: Okay.

JIM: That's a very basic email teaser and that is something you could have done ahead of time for your JV partners to adapt and use.

Here's a link to an email teaser that has worked very well for us: **http://www.7DayeBook.com/emails.shtml**

DAVID: **Okay, so to sum it up, you're giving your potential JV partner the teaser, your telling him he's going to make x number of dollars per unit sold and your going to show him proven copy from your website which has a conversion rate of a certain number of sales per one hundred (100) visitors?**

JIM: Exactly. Your going to make it idiot simple for that potential joint venture partner to say, "Wow! I've got 10,000 people on my list and if I could get 3,000 people to show up to this person's website, then we're going to sell 90-180 of them, and I would make between $1,100 and $2,300."

DAVID: **Very good.**

JIM: And then they could evaluate right there, either "I'll do it" or "I won't do it". What some of them will do is they will test a small ad in their ezine or they'll do some other kind of small test to see how their list responds to the offer. If it does well, then they will go ahead and do what's called "roll it out" to their list.

But by presenting all that information right up front to the potential joint venture partner, you present yourself as a very professional person, someone who has their act together… and you massively increase your chances of having someone work with you.

DAVID: **That sounds great. Okay, anything else you can do to further motivate them to move on your offer and say "Yes" to working with you?**

JIM: One of the things that really works with a lot of joint-venture partners is giving them the opportunity to play what I call the "Santa Claus" Role. The people you are most interested in working with are very interested in improving and enhancing the relationship that they have with their list.

HOT TIP So if you can go to a potential joint-venture partner and say to them, "Hey, not only am I going to let you offer my ebook for a BIG commissions, but I'm also going to throw in an extra bonus that isn't even available on my website" or

"I'll extend the guarantee by another sixty (60) days and you can tell people, 'Hey, you've got ninety (90) days to try this out'" or

"I'll give you the opportunity to offer your people a special discounted price for a limited time" or

"I'm offering it on my website for $39.00, but I'll let you offer it to your list for $29.00 for as long as you want to sell it."

Anything that you can do to use the Santa Claus thing, especially if you don't have a list!

I marketed a step-by-step information tutorial product on CD where we didn't have our own list, so, quite frankly, it didn't matter what we were selling it for on our site because we didn't have any of our own customers to sell it to.

HOT TIP So what we did was we priced the CD on our own website at $199.00, but then we let all of our affiliates and all of our joint-venture partners offer it for $97.00!

They sent their people to a special page, and in effect, on that page it said, "Hey, you don't believe this is a special deal, you don't believe that I worked my butt off to get this for you for half price? Go ahead and look at the main page of their website and see how much you will pay".

We sold about $100,000.00 worth of them in about four and one half (4 ½) months, mostly all through other people's lists. A big part of the reason that I was able to do that was because they were able to play "Santa Claus" to their list by giving them this "great deal". Plus we had proven copy, plus we had a better guarantee, and overall made it so attractive to those JV partners financially AND we solved a major problem for their audience!

It was such a great deal all the way around that the vast majority of them pushed it for us with great success!

DAVID: **WOW! Let's keep talking about joint venture partners.**

How do you pay them? How does that work?

JIM: You pay them fast… you pay them well… and you pay them on time! One of the questions that I get asked a lot is how much do I pay my joint venture partners.

My rule of thumb is that if you're selling a download product, a product that can be totally delivered by remote control, requires no intervention on your part, and once it's setup on a website, people just show up and purchase, then I always pay fifty percent (50%).

DAVID: **Is that fifty (50%) percent of the purchase price or fifty (50%) percent after the transaction fee?**

JIM: I use **ClickBank** so it ends up being fifty percent (50%) <u>after</u> the transaction fees. But, however you phrase it, you need to pay fifty percent (50%) after whatever fees and you need to tell people exactly what that means.

Now, with a big enough joint-venture partner, you say to them, "I'll pay you 50% and I'll eat the fees. I'll pay you a straight 50% of the sales price!"

If you can get somebody who has 100,000 people on their list to endorse your ebook, and it's a targeted market, and it's a very focused offer — an offer that meets a very pressing and burning need — you could end up selling 500 or 1000 ebooks at one shot!

DAVID: **That's a lot of Ebooks!**

JIM: Yes it is… and that's why you pay your joint venture partners 50 percent! And if they are big enough, you just pay them a straight 50 percent and you eat the fees… if you're smart.

Because what they're doing when they do an endorsed mailing is they are sending their best customers to you. They know that! So you need to use the money as the final piece of the puzzle to make it a no-brainer for them to endorse your product.

DAVID: **Well, you know, I can see this question coming up. I'm an author, and boy, I put a lot of work into this ebook.**

Fifty percent seems like a lot of money to give up! Am I going to make money that way if I'm giving up so much of my purchase price?

JIM: Well, half of something is a whole lot better than all of <u>nothing</u>. And what is going to motivate somebody who's got a list? …I mean, this is a business! What is going to motivate somebody who's got a list is paying them half the sales price on a download product that will help them build their relationship with their list. Not only will they make money endorsing your product, but they will also be seen as a resource for new and good product information by their list.

Unless you have a list and can trade mailings, you use the money as your main motivator.

By the way, when I say 50 percent, I'm talking about a $29, $39, $49 ebook.

When things start getting up there in price — say $400 to $1,000 e-classes and things like that — then you can start thinking in terms of just a flat fee like $100. But I know very well established marketers who will tell you right up front, "We don't mail on anything unless we're going to make at least $50 per unit sold."

HOT TIP So you need to make it financially worth their while because your end-run objective with everything you're doing is to end up with your own list!

Why? Because everyone who buys from you is going to go on your list! In a later section we'll show you how to set up a fully automated ebook delivery system, part of which is collecting people's names and emails in and auto-responder so you can send them sales messages automatically. Once these people are on your list, you keep all the commission if they buy something else.

Also, by setting up a pop-up window offering a free mini-course or some other incentive on exit (we'll talk more on that later) you will capture some of the names and emails of people who don't buy from you right away, but might buy later after they hear from you a few times with quality information.

So, you see, one of the key benefits (to me the most important benefit) of working with joint venture partners is not only that you will make sales, but if you set up your site the right way, you will add a significant number of the people they send to your site to your own list!

Why is this so great? Because with your own list you are the one sending the emails and keeping ALL the commission — in the case of your own products — or you can send emails about other people's products and take half the commission for doing little more than just sending an email.

By the way, the best list you can have is a list of people who have bought from you in the past, but a list of people who sign up for your free mini-course but don't buy right away is still a great list to have.

So don't look at the commission percentage with joint venture partners as this huge chunk you have to pay — look at it as a very reasonable price to pay for selling lots of ebooks and building up your own list so you can do your own mailings in the future.

This is the exact technique I have used to build my lists well into the 5 figures in less than a year! Paying your joint venture partners this way is your "ticket" to get into the game.

DAVID: **Okay, if you can get 50 percent of the dollar amount on sales from that customer the first time, then you will get 100% of the sale from them if you're selling them your next product because they're on your own list now?**

JIM: You are absolutely right. And that is how you go from zero on your list to over twelve thousand people on your various ebook lists in less than a year.

DAVID: **Mm hm. Do you bring that up for a particular reason?**

JIM: Yeah, because that's what I've done.

DAVID: **[laugh] I see. Not bad. Let's move on to the next section…**

Section 2

The Secret of Fast Cash

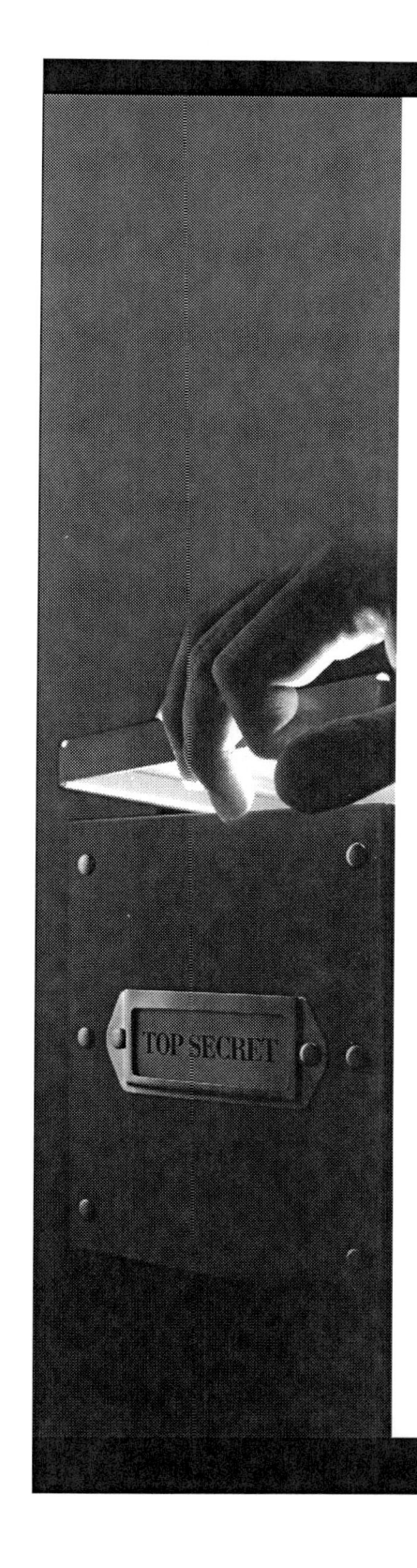

The Secret of Fast Cash
SECTION 2

DAVID: **All right, let's talk about resale rights.**

JIM: Okay. Resale rights — as far as ebooks go — are the way to pile up the money the fastest because, if you remember those ten reasons I told you people buy anything, <u>the number one reason anybody buys anything is to make money</u>.

And if somebody is very interested in your ebook, and they want to turn around and resell it, and they think that they can make a lot of money, then instead of paying you $19, $29, $39 for your ebook, they'll pay you $100, $200, $300 for the right to resell your ebook and keep all the profits.

And the money piles up a lot faster when people are paying you $100, $200, $300 a pop than if you are collecting it at $29 a pop.

DAVID: **So you mean I could write an ebook and instead of selling an individual copy, I would sell a license that allows someone to resell the ebook?**

JIM: Yes. But that only really works well if you've got your own list — or you've got a joint venture partner who's got a list, and that partner has absolutely no interest whatsoever in buying the resale rights themselves and handling any of the sales aspect of selling your ebook.

Here's what I mean: Anyone who could be a potential joint venture partner for you will have this question right off the bat if you're selling resale rights to your ebook. They'll ask "Why would I sell this as an affiliate or as a joint venture partner and only get half the ebook sale when I could buy the resale rights myself, sell this book to my list, and keep **all** the money?"

DAVID: **So the chances are good that selling "resale rights" is really going to work only if you have your own list 90 percent of the time.**

JIM: Not necessarily. If you can find a joint venture partner that doesn't want to mess around with setting up a shopping cart, setting up to take the money, setting up to deliver the ebook, answering technical support questions or doing all the things that are necessary to sell and deliver an ebook online.

And believe it or not, there are actually quite a number people out there like that who have lists but don't want to get into the technical part of delivering an ebook.

DAVID: **But isn't the same thing going to be necessary for them to sell with resale rights as it is to sell the ebook as a joint venture partner?**

JIM: Yes, but it comes down to who is doing all the work and providing the setup to actually sell the ebook.

If you are doing all the work in a joint venture, then basically all your partner has to do is send an email to their group. You will answer customer questions, handle sales, issue refunds, provide technical assistances etc.

If they buy the resale rights then the list owner has to take care of all those details. Some list owners don't want to or aren't set up for that… and quite frankly a lot of them would rather just send the email and take half the money and be done with it.

DAVID: **Oh, I see. I see what you're saying. If they were to sell it on their own — not as a joint venture partner, but if they were to buy the resale rights and then sell individual copies of the book to people on their list — then they would have to set up the mechanics of delivering the ebooks 100 percent themselves.**

JIM: Right. And many ezine publishers are not interested in doing that. Someone that is already selling ebooks or electronic products online is probably going to be more interested in purchasing the resale rights and then selling the book, because they already have the equipment and the know-how. They'll easily be able to set up to sell the ebook themselves and keep all the profits.

HOT TIP But if you set it up right, in the book you put a link that anybody who buys the book from a reseller has to come back to you to buy the resale rights for themselves… and that is how it gets viral across the Internet.

CAUTION: Make it very clear to people who buy resale rights from you that they do not have "Master" Resale rights, meaning they can't sell resale rights to others. They can only resell the ebook and keep all the profits. Unless you have a really good reason (and I can't think of one), you want to be the only one selling resale rights because that is where the big money is.

DAVID: **All right. Now, have people made a lot of money quickly selling resale rights?**

JIM: Oh yes!

DAVID: Do you have any specifics?

JIM: Well, with "33 Days To Online Profits", we've made a significant amount of money selling resale rights. We sell two levels of resale rights: one is called the Silver level, which people buy for $99.00, and they can resell the book all they want and keep the $29.00.

And we sell the Gold resale rights for $299.00 where we customize all the affiliate links in the book with their affiliate links so they create a backend path of income stream out of the ebook.

In both cases, anyone who wants to buy resale rights must buy them from us… we don't sell "master resale" rights.

DAVID: And you sell a lot of these?

JIM: Yes. We did over $42,000 in business the first month and have gotten up into a healthy six-figure amount in the last 6 months with the sales still coming in.

DAVID: WOW! That's a good number.

What are the downsides of resale rights?

JIM: As with anything that sounds this good, there is a downside.

With resale rights you can lose control over how your ebook gets distributed, and as much as you want to create a license or try and control what people do with it, when somebody halfway around the world buys the resale rights to your book, they're going to do whatever they want. And there's really nothing you can do to stop them.

For example, your ebook will show up for sale on e-Bay. Or, people will start giving it away. So then you'll have people that paid for the resale rights all of a sudden showing up whining to you that "Oh, somebody's selling it for $3 and there's no way I can charge $29 if so-and-so is only charging $3. I want my money back."

What they don't realize is there's something like 200 million people or however many out there on the Internet. The chances of people finding that deal, especially since somebody who's selling it for $3 is not going to have any money to promote it with, it's not really that big of a deal — but that's the kind of stuff that happens.

In extreme cases, people will try and take credit for writing your ebook. They'll modify your sales letter and take credit for it. They'll do all sorts of crazy stuff. And that's the downside.

But the upside is you can make a whole lot of money really fast.

DAVID: **Is there anything you have to be careful of, like guarantees or anything?**

JIM: Well, with regard to the book itself or the sales letter, not really. The resellers take the money and they have to honor whatever guarantees are made in the sales letter.

You need to make sure that whatever guarantees you make, like with a customized version of your ebook (our Gold resale rights), be very careful to let people know that it's a non-refundable purchase. Once we've customized the book with their affiliate links we can't really take it back. So, you have to let them know that it's non-refundable.

DAVID: Okay.

JIM: And you just have to clearly spell out what their resale rights are so that if somebody starts violating their agreement with you, you can send them a cease and desist letter.

But realistically, whether they stop or not, as soon as they're outside the U.S. there's very little you can do to enforce an agreement.

Section 3

How to Build Your Own List

How to Build Your Own List
SECTION 3

DAVID: **All right. Let's move on to the question of having your own list.**

You've said before that the real thing that you're going for by and large is your own list. That's the end result you want, and that's the reason you're willing to give up so much of the purchase price of the book.

Tell me about that.

JIM: Well basically, the "power is in the list", or like my buddy Larry Chase says, "the power is in the pipes" — the distribution. It's almost like having a private license to print money!

Because if you have the ear of, say, 10,000 people, or 5,000 people, who you know are interested in a specific topic or a certain niche market subject, once you've got them, then you can be the one to roll out your own or other people's products to them... and make half the commission on an ebook, e-product, software package, or a service that you have nothing to do with creating or delivering.

In the case of endorsing someone else's product, all you're doing is making the audience aware of it and getting paid for sending the email.

The fastest way to build your list is by collecting the names and email addresses of the people who buy your ebook and then sending them value-added follow-up messages such as articles, tips and tricks and other content they are very interested in.

Another way to build your list quickly is to capture the names and emails of people who come to your site but don't buy right away. You send them really good information to build your relationship with them and you also send them sales pitches for yours and other people's products.

The most effective way to capture their names and email is using an exit pop-up window that offers a mini-course or a free report that gives them more information about the subject of your ebook.

A great example is the exit pop-up window on the 7 day ebook site (http://www.eBookSecretsExposed.com/7dayebook.html) that offers a mini-course on writing your own ebook. If you visit the site and then leave without clicking the "order" link or the "earn money" link then you will see an exit pop-up offering a free course on creating a profitable ebook. About 10% of the people who don't buy sign up for that free course.

Those are the two fastest ways to build up your lists when working with joint venture partners.

The <u>reward</u> for all this — when you do write another book or create another info product, then <u>you just roll it out to your own list</u>!

They already know you, trust you, like you, and have bought from you in the past. So if you write a book that's properly researched and created for their specific needs, wants and desires, then you should make a whole bunch of sales real fast... and you get to keep all the money!

DAVID: **Okay. That sounds good. But, you know, the one area I'm stuck on is you say you have to go to a joint**

venture partner, including the first one you ever approach, with some "proven copy", with your conversion numbers.

But how can you get those numbers to begin with without going to a joint venture partner.... it sort of sounds like which came first, the chicken or the egg?

How do you get these numbers so you can go find joint venture partners in the first place if you don't even have a list?

JIM: Excellent question!

The way that you do that is by using pay-per-click search engines or with ezine classified ads... or you really twist the arm of a friend. If you've got a friend with a list that's in your target audience, you just twist their arm, literally.

But if you don't have any friends and you don't have anybody that you know who can mail for you, then you need to go to www.Overture.com or www.findwhat.com and you need to buy some pay-per-click search engine listings so that you can run three, four, five, six hundred to a thousand people across your web site to see if people will buy.

Use that traffic to see what kind of numbers convert... how many people that show up actually buy your ebook.

Don't worry too much about what you spend per click right now because at this point you want to get the traffic really fast so you can see if your sales letter needs to be tweaked.

DAVID: **Okay. That's fair. How about the search engines where you don't pay?**

JIM: The search engines where you don't pay are getting tougher to use and are actually disappearing.

The problem with search engines is that <u>if</u> they'll index your pages, and <u>if</u> your pages are made the right way, and <u>if</u> you submit them to the right search engines that still take free listings, it takes weeks if not months to get any results — positive or negative. <u>You can't get the results fast enough</u> to test your copy to get your numbers in order to approach joint venture partners.

By the way, there's a whole industry that surrounds search engine promotion. So it's not just something you can just "decide" to do one day… it takes a lot of study, time and whole lot of trial and error.

You can also buy ads in ezines for $15-35 and test your offer that way in just a few days. Most ezines are always looking for advertisers. Make sure, if possible, that you buy a "Top Sponsorship" ad, which means your ad appears first in the publication. Ads at the bottom don't get read nearly as much as ads at the top of the page.

So the way you solve your "chicken and the egg" problem is through buying some pay-per-click traffic and some ezine classified ads to get visitors fast. Once that traffic starts coming you want to keep a close eye on your sales letter's conversion rate.

The way to figure your conversion rate for your sales letter is to look at your website statistics — almost every web hosting account comes with them. Make sure you read the help file on your hosting account to find out exactly how the "stats" work because they are all a little different. At this point, the one statistic you care about the most is "unique visitors".

"Unique visitors" are different from "clicks", which usually means how many times your page was viewed. One unique visitor might represent 2, 3 or even more clicks over time. You need to know how many unique individuals have been to your site in a given period of time?

NOTE: Some website statistics accounts reset every day so you need to find out exactly how the stats work, how they report and when and if they reset themselves automatically.

To figure your conversion rate for your sales letter you simply divide the number of sales by the number of unique visitors in a given time.

Let's say you advertise your website for two weeks using pay-per-click traffic and a couple of ezine ads. At the end of two weeks you have made 9 sales and you've had 1089 unique visitors. That means your sales letter has a conversion factor of .8% — not that great, but not terrible.

You would next want to test a different headline or tweak your offer until you got the conversion rate up as high as you could.

Let's say you test a new headline for another 2 weeks. This time you have made 14 sales to 997 unique visitors. That's a conversion factor of 1.4% — you're getting there.

Now, you decide to double your money back guarantee period from 30 days to 60 and you throw in another bonus. You run for another week and have 13 sales from 653 unique visitors. That's a conversion rate of 1.99% — I would start looking for joint venture partners fast!

DAVID: **Okay, so that's sort of a secondary strategy. If we're talking about making money fast, maybe your first step really is the pay-per-click search engines or the ezine classifieds, because you're going to know very soon what your numbers are.**

JIM: Exactly. You're going to know very soon whether or not your sales letter converts lookers into buyers. And the other thing to keep in mind is that's really some of the crummiest traffic that you can get.

If you can convert off of pay-per-click search engine traffic or ezine classified ad traffic, then with somebody who endorses your ebook to a list of people they know and tells them "Hey, you should go check out Jim's book, because it does this, this, this, and this, and he gave us a special price on it," you should be able to convert a whole heck of a lot more of those people into buyers.

DAVID: **Excellent point... let's talk about pricing next....**

Section 4

How to Price Your eBook for Maximum Profit

How to Price Your eBook for Maximum Profit
SECTION 4

DAVID: **Okay. What about pricing? How do I roll out my ebook at the proper price point for maximum sales at the highest price?**

JIM: That's one of the most frequent questions I get asked, "How should I price my ebook?"

The answer to that is several-fold, and the first step is to go and look and see what price other people are selling similar products for.

So if you see out there that somebody's selling a product that looks like it's directly competitive with what you offer and they're selling it for 19 bucks and somebody else is out there selling something <u>very similar</u> for $15 or for $29… you can feel confident the range for that product is somewhere between $19-$30.

Unless you have something so unique and different, then that's the price range where you're probably going to end up.

If you go out there and prices are all over the board, then what you always need to do is start low and work your way up.

The last thing you ever want to do is start high and then start working your way down… especially if you are making some sales and then keep reducing the price down. If you do it in a short enough period of time, people who bought at the higher price are usually going to want to get their money back if they find out about the reduction.

DAVID: **Yeah.**

JIM: So, you need to be careful with that. Now if you offer it at $97 and nobody buys or two people buy, I wouldn't worry too much about lowering the price and making those couple of people angry.

And then once you get down around $49 or $59 or wherever in that range your ebook starts to sell in any real quantities, then you can start looking to see what appears to be the right price — the right balance of units sold vs. price.

But the first step is see what other people are getting or "appear" to be getting for the ebooks they are selling.

DAVID: **Do you have any rules of thumb?**

JIM: There is a pricing "formula" or really a strategy that I like to use. What I like to do is to send out a pre-announcement to my own list, or to a list of people that know me, or to a list of people that trust the person who's sending it out (a JV partner) that I probably have a really good relationship with.

And let's say I'm going to ultimately sell this book for between $29 and $49. The first thing I'll do is have a pre-launch price of say $25. I'll explain why in a minute.

DAVID: **Okay.**

JIM: And that "pre-launch" price is only good for three or four days. And then on the fourth day I raise the price up to $29 and then I have the "official" announcement.

And if I get really, really good results from that "official" announcement, and what I mean by good results is 5 to 10 percent of the people buy (but maybe even 4 to 7 percent is good), then I'm going to raise the price again up to $39.

DAVID: **What do you do next?**

JIM: From there, I'm going to pretty much hold it around $39 to see how my conversion rate does. If I keep finding joint venture partners or other people, like affiliates, to mail on it and if it's still selling like hotcakes with a high conversion, then I'm going to raise the price again to $49 and keep testing the price.

Eventually I'll reach a point of equilibrium.

If I go from a price of $29 up to $39 sales might start to slack off. What I care about is that I'm still making more money because I might be selling fewer total units, but I'm making more money <u>total</u> than at the lower price.

Wherever the breakpoint is I'll pretty much leave it there… but then I'll threaten to raise it even more, usually in the P.S. section of the sales letter.

DAVID: **Why do you do that?**

JIM: It works better that way. See, I've always got that threat under there to raise the price. "I could raise this to $49 any time I want…." But if I had it at $29 originally and I raised it up to $39 and sales really fall off, then I'd just drop it back down to $29 and threaten to raise it to $39 or $49.

DAVID: **That makes sense.**

JIM: So, here's the kicker... the reason that I offer it for that pre-launch price of $25 is first, to try and really entice or to reward the early action takers. That's number 1.

HOT TIP And number 2, I want to prove to people on my list or somebody else's that I'm serious about raising the price. They can't get it for $25 any more and they better act now before I decide to raise it again!

DAVID: So they're afraid if you've already done it once you might do it again.

JIM: Exactly!

DAVID: That's a great strategy.

JIM: It works very well!

DAVID: Anything else?

JIM: Yes. Here's another reason you'd really rather start low and work your way up in price rather than to start high and work your way down.

By starting high and working your way down, what are you going to do, go back three weeks later to the exact same list and say "Oh, yeah, we tried to gouge you for 79 bucks, but now we're offering it for $29. Are you interested?"

I don't think so!

DAVID: Right.

JIM: You can't really give that kind of a pitch. That doesn't work very well at all.

But a cool pitch is to say, "Hey, we offered it for three days at $25. Now we raised it up to $29… and you'd better act fast because I'm going to raise it up to $39 really soon!" And then if you do actually raise it up to $39 and it keeps selling, then they're really freaking — they're scrambling to get it before you raise the price again.

Section 5

How to Make More Money With Your eBook

How to Make More Money With Your eBook
SECTION 5

DAVID: **All right, so I have a pretty good idea of the basics of making a lot of money with sales of the ebook itself, but what I'd like to know now is, suppose I'm making money but I'd like to make some more money. How can I make more money with my ebook customers, especially without spending more money on advertising or on pay-per-click traffic?**

JIM: There are two ways that you can make extra money without spending any more money on advertising or on traffic.

The first one is through "back end" sales, and there are two types of back end sales. The first type is through the ebook itself. If you've ever read one of my ebooks or if you've ever looked at one of my ebooks, you know that there are usually a ton of links in them. All those links go to resources, more information, related websites — and they also go to something else…

They go to tools that will help you do something even better, more in-depth, or more extensively than I might be able to tell you about in the ebook.

DAVID: **What's an example of a tool?**

JIM: An example of a tool? Okay, let me tell you the book that has done the best as far as back end sales from links in the book has been the "33 Days to Online Profits". And the reason it's done so well is because that ebook is laid out as a 33-day step-by-step, paint by numbers guide to launching virtually any business on the Internet.

And no matter what business you want to be in on the Internet, there are certain things that you <u>must</u> have. Those things are web site hosting, a domain name, autoresponder, shopping cart, credit card merchant account, graphics, a little bit of web work, a web site, affiliate program and all these different things you must have.

DAVID: **Those are tools?**

JIM: Those are tools that are woven into the book itself. I mean, you can't do what we tell you in the book without having these tools, but you also can't do anything else online without them either.

DAVID: **Now, how do you make money with this?**

JIM: We have our affiliate links in there as the links people click on in the ebooks.

DAVID: **Oh, okay, I see. So the book's like a little cash register for you.**

JIM: It has done very well, and the back end sales on that actually beat out the total ebook sales of my *For Sale by Owner* book every month. Just the sales that are made from the affiliate links in that book.

And again, because we've sold the resale rights and we've got hundreds of people out there selling the book that wasn't customized, those are all our affiliate links in the books they are selling too! Remember I told you we sell resale rights on 2 levels? The first level they sell an ebook that has our back-end links in there making us money!

DAVID: **Explain that a little more.**

JIM: Well, on the first level, they're selling the book, but all the links in there are customized with our links. So there are thousands of people out there reading that ebook and if they buy something through the ebook we get paid a commission!

DAVID: **Wait just a minute! Hold the phone!**

You just said something that, you just sorta said it glibly, it slipped by, but you said it's doing better than the total sales of your *For Sale by Owner* ebook. You mean you're making more money with the back end out of the affiliate links from the *33 Days* book per month than you are with the other book which pays your house payment, pays both your cars and pays your electric bill?

JIM: That is correct.

DAVID: **My goodness!**

JIM: But the thing is, you've got to do it right. And let me tell you how to do it right…

The way to do it is to be very subtle about it and to really integrate the links with the book. And it's more an art than it is a science. They've got to be what we call "in context" links. You can't just say, "Oh, you're going to need a web site hosting account, here's this, this, this and this" and expect to get paid. People can find hosting offers all over the web — they don't need you to give them a list of links.

What you've got to do is say, "Okay, you're going to need a web site hosting account. Here's what to look for in one. Here are the criteria for what makes a good web site hosting account. Here are the considerations that you're going to need to pay attention to. And here are nine different hosting accounts grouped by how much they charge you each month. So if you're on a tight budget you can choose from these, and these are the advantages and these are the disadvantages..." and so on and so forth.

DAVID: **I see. You provide information, not just blanket recommendations.**

JIM: Right. You can't just throw links into your ebook and think that people are going to buy.

HOT TIP
You have to add value by helping people understand how and why those links benefit them within the context of the ebook as they are reading. You have to build trust by making them understand that you recommend, endorse or have fully evaluated the link they are going to click and they can feel comfortable making a purchase.

DAVID: **And each one of the ones you recommend has an affiliate program?**

JIM: That is correct.

DAVID: **That's very clever. Okay. What else can you do with back end sales?**

82 eBook Secrets EXPOSED

JIM: Well, remember I told you that you want to build your list of people who have bought from you?

DAVID: Right.

JIM: Well someone who's bought from you trusts your opinion and what you say.

DAVID: Sure.

JIM: So the other part of the back end, and I've mentioned this before, but we'll say it again, is being able to <u>recommend other people's products and other people's services to your own list</u>. And usually all you've got to do to make money with that is send out an email!

If you've got competent, smart people approaching you to do joint ventures, they'll pretty much show up with a proven email in hand. Then all you have to do is just adapt the email message somewhat for your list to fit the "tone" they're used to hearing from you, and you send it out and make money!

When done correctly, this is a beautiful thing!

DAVID: So that list is really valuable, because you're going to be able to make money even without coming up with a new ebook.

JIM: That list, in the end, is the most valuable asset you have. It is, like I said, practically a private license to print money.

DAVID: Interesting.

JIM: Without a doubt, and I'm going to say that again…

HOT TIP The list you build up of people who have either bought from you or subscribe to your free mini-course, those people on that list who hear from you, know you, trust you, and stay on your list — that list is the most important asset in your business!

Ultimately what it turns into, if you really want to grow it and get big with this, is that you spend your time not only looking for new customers for your own list, but also looking for new products or creating new products for your customers to buy from you. The list becomes your business!

DAVID: That's good. Now, there's something known as "up-selling", and the classic example most people are familiar with from McDonald's is the line, "Do you want fries with that?" But on the Internet I guess it's "Do you want to buy this additional (whatever) along with your ebook?" Could you talk about up-selling?

JIM: Well, basically up-selling is an offer for the purchase of an additional item that you make to the customer at the point of purchase, or shortly thereafter.

You can ask somebody if they would like to buy more of something they're already purchasing. A good example of that is somebody goes to a web site to buy vitamins. You could offer them another 30-day supply at 40 percent off, because the money that you make from that is all pure profit. You have no money invested in customer acquisition; they're standing there already buying.

With information products and with ebooks, the upsell is a little bit tougher. With an ebook, you've got to be careful that you don't scare them off because all of a sudden you jump the sale from $29, $39 or $49 up to $79, $89 real fast.

One of the things that works real well as an upsell is software, especially a software program that quickly accomplishes something that is outlined in the your ebook.

A lot of online marketers who sell ebooks about marketing on the Internet sell software that helps you submit to the search engines or to submit your classified ads to free sites, or manage your contact list. Really anything that helps people accomplish something you teach them in your ebook better, faster, cheaper or easier than without it works well as an upsell for an ebook.

But you also have to be careful and sometimes it's hard to say what would be a good upsell. Let me give you an example of one that initially we thought about, but then we backed off from. This was with the seven day ebook, "How to Write and Publish Your Own eBook in as little as Seven Days", which is really a book about <u>writing</u> an ebook that gives you a taste of marketing.

DAVID: **Yes.**

JIM: A natural thought that we had was "Hey, we'll upsell with an ebook compiler, that makes sense." Sell them a program to help somebody easily put together and package up an ebook.

But then upon closer inspection we realized that the majority of those ebook compilers don't work with Macintosh computers. (In fact, I've never seen an ebook compiler that does.)

And so, to me, what you're doing there by selling an ebook compiler that doesn't work with a Mac — at least to me — is selling somebody something that's going to cause them problems when they sell their ebook to Mac owners and then realize it doesn't work.

Yikes! Talk about potential trouble.

Plus I'm a big believer in selling your ebooks in PDF format because it's stable and it works on virtually any computer that's still running today.

DAVID: **Right.**

JIM: So for that particular product we've never really found anything that makes a great upsell... so we don't currently have an upsell for that. But our back-end rocks with more sales of additional ebooks and offers, so I'm happy with it.

An up-sell is a tricky thing. I know marketers that I trust, and I know they've sold a lot more ebooks than I have, who do not offer up-sells at the initial purchase. They feel like it drives people away. They think you should grab the sale they came for and then sell more on the back end once this one is "in the bag".

DAVID: **So when is it a good idea to up-sell?**

JIM: Under the right circumstances, if it's very natural, if it's a very good extension of the original purchase, then an up-sell can make you a LOT of extra money.

A fantastic example of it working in outrageously successful fashion is the "33 Days to Online Profits" ebook. About 1/3 of the people who purchase that ebook up-sell to the "Silver" resale rights package at the point of purchase. In other words, <u>1 in 3 goes from a $29 purchase to a $99 purchase</u>!

HOT TIP Upselling resale rights to your ebook is an AWESOME upsell, because it is a natural extension of the original purchase!

I will tell you another one that I know works VERY well as an up-sell.

DAVID: **Yeah?**

JIM: It's Yanik Silver with his **Instant Sales Letter.** Click Here → **http://www.eBookSecretsExposed.com/isl.html**

He has an upsell that does great!

Yanik sells a really incredible service called *Instant Sales Letters,* which gives you letter templates that sell very well. As you go through the purchase process he up-sells you a book he found, some "lost" manuscript that a pioneering copy writer wrote back in the late 1800's or early 1900's that's all about writing sales letters.

By the way, it's a really good book!

Yanik will sell you a copy of it for like $10 extra. Well, you're already signing up for Instant Sales Letters for only $39. For only an extra 10 or 15 bucks you get this book, plus he throws in even more stuff with the up-sell. Most people say, "Yeah, what the heck! I'll go for it" and take the upsell.

He up-sells a lot of them. Plus, it doesn't hurt that he has an awesome product!

DAVID: **That always helps.**

JIM: But an upsell is a tricky thing, so don't just slap something up there and expect extra revenue to magically come to you. But, if you put a lot of thought into it and test various offers, it can bring you massive amounts of extra money without spending a single extra dime to bring more visitors to your site.

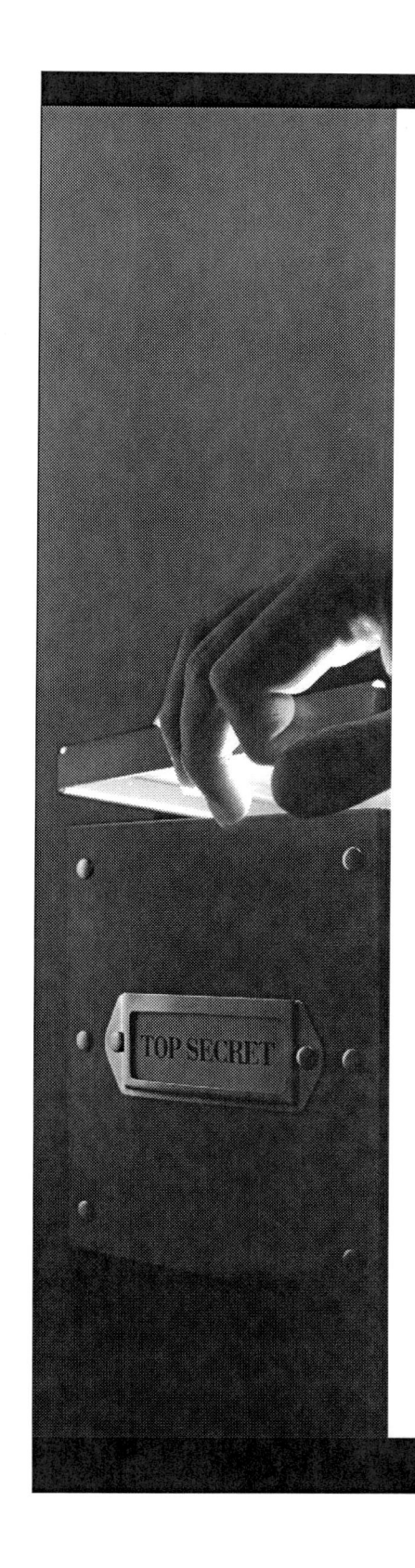

Section 6

Heading Off Potential Problems

Heading Off Potential Problems
SECTION 6

DAVID: **Okay. What about problems?**

We've talked about a lot of things: business arrangements, marketing techniques, making more money... a lot of really great stuff!

Tell me what kind of problems are going to come up, and what's the solution to each problem you mention?

JIM: Well, the number one problem that's going to come up is that it's never going to happen as fast as you want it to.

DAVID: **And the solution?**

JIM: The solution to that is to always keep your eye on the goal and keep your mind focused on what you want until you get through to it, because your first ebook is probably going to be the hardest.

DAVID: **All right.**

JIM: So just <u>accept</u> the fact that it's not going to happen overnight. But it can happen really fast. It can even happen in a couple weeks.

DAVID: **All right. What other problems?**

JIM: The other problem is that it takes perseverance!

Once you've got the ebook together, the web site together and you've tested your copy and done everything, the first joint venture partner you contact probably isn't going to do business with you. You're going to have to contact 10, 15, 20, 30, 40. As many as it takes to get one to do business with you!

DAVID: You have to contact that many to get a yes?

JIM: Maybe the first one will jump on it. Maybe you've got the jewel they've been looking for or that makes so much sense to sell to their list that they are stumbling all over themselves to get your book out to their list.

The bottom-line is, you've just got to persevere until it happens.

DAVID: Any other problems?

JIM: Another problem that you're going to run into is, unless you understand how to set up a web site, how to set up autoresponders, how to set up all the mechanics yourself, there's going to be a learning curve.

I can sit here and explain to you how to swim. I can tell you there's water over there and you jump in and you move your arms a certain way and you kick your feet a certain way and you can get across to the other side of the pool. But <u>until you actually jump in the water and do it</u>, that's when the real learning actually takes place.

DAVID: Right.

JIM: So you're going to have to jump in <u>and you're just going to have to do it</u> and you're going to have to take your licks and

				learn the mechanics to either do it yourself or you're going to have to hire somebody to do it for you.

DAVID: **All right. Any other problems I should be aware of before I jump into this?**

JIM: I think the biggest one — the one that you need to be vigilant about — is that it's an internal process that you're going to go through, and let me explain that. This business has got such a low cost of entry, what other business can you start for a couple hundred bucks? For a couple hundred dollars you can get this thing rolling down the trail.

DAVID: **How does that affect the entrepreneur?**

JIM:

HOT TIP

Well, people get these big expectations and they think that they're going to get rich overnight... and typically that doesn't happen overnight. My goals are not to have two or three ebooks that are making me $10,000 a month each. I would rather have ten ebooks that are making me $3,000 a month each.

You must understand it's a commitment to a process. The people who are looking at this to make them rich overnight <u>without any effort</u> are really in for a tough row to hoe. But if you will commit to the process, learn what's necessary and take these invaluable insights that we're giving you in this course and you'll apply them, then you should do fine.

Actually, you should do more than fine — **you should dominate your niche market**! But it's not going to happen overnight. It can, but it's probably won't.

DAVID: **Maybe not overnight, but some things really could happen in two to four weeks.**

JIM: Oh, absolutely. If good things <u>don't</u> start happening in two to four weeks. you haven't done something right.

DAVID: Well, results and profitability in two to four weeks is pretty much overnight compared to most businesses. I mean, look how long it took amazon.com to turn its first profit!

JIM: [laugh] Sure. Absolutely!

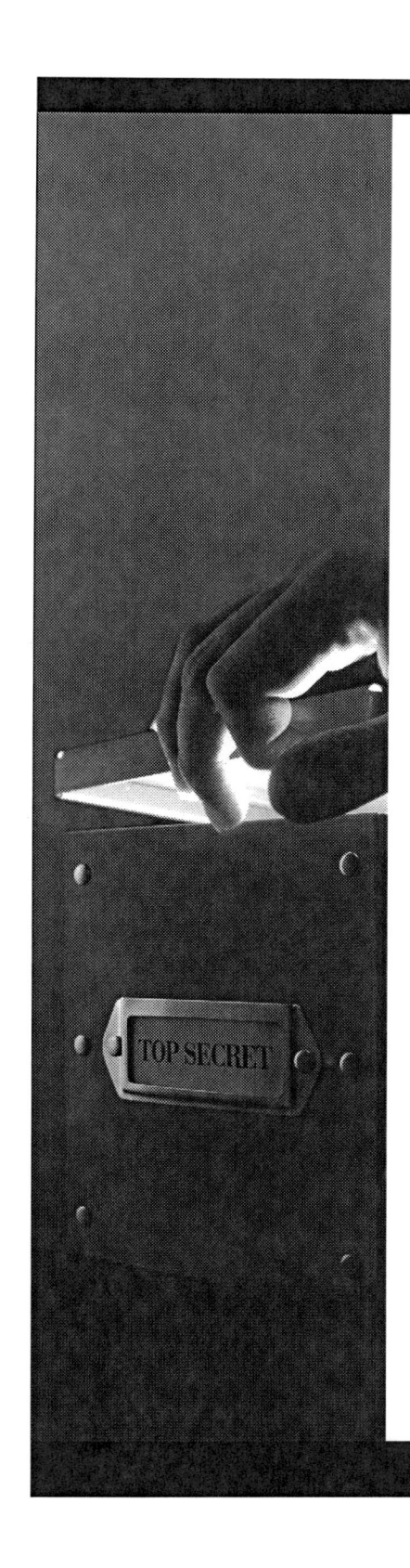

Section 7

The Heart-Breaking Mistake Most Authors Make

The Heart-Breaking Mistake Most Authors Make
SECTION 7

DAVID: **Horror stories. What can happen if you don't have the information we're teaching people in this ebook?**

JIM: Okay. Here's the number one mistake... and you can take all the scenarios you want from this number one mistake that people make.

And that is writing an ebook and investing months if not years of your life writing what you consider a book without giving any thought to who is going to buy it!

Then you get to the end and find out that nobody wanted it but you, or that you can't contact the potential market in a cost-effective manner.

So even worse, you've got a book that people would buy if you could market it, the problem is that you don't have any way to market it to the people who could buy it!

What makes this so heart-breaking is that as you're creating an ebook, especially if it's your first one, you'll naturally start looking at it as something that's going to "save you" from whatever circumstances you're in. If you're short of money, it's going to be the thing that's going to make you a lot of money.

If you're in a crappy job, it's going to be the thing that's going to help you get out from under a crappy job or from boss who doesn't appreciate you. The ebook is going to be a way for you to finally get out into the world and people are going to know who you are — you're going to be famous — you're going to make money — only to have those hopes dashed and totally destroyed on the rocks of reality because you didn't do a few hours worth of due diligence.

You didn't take a few hours to see if there was going to be a cheap and easy way for you to market this ebook.

You didn't take the time to identify a whole bunch of potential joint venture partners ahead of time so you knew you'd be able to find someone to help you roll out your book.

You didn't research the market to see if there was anybody out there who would buy this book from you and so you end up with something that nobody buys and you're totally disappointed and destroyed by life.

That, my friend, is a horror story many people have lived and it stinks!

DAVID: **Whoa... I think that is a horror story anyone who is reading this ebook has gotten a clear and definite message they need to avoid at all costs. WOW!**

Okay. Let me ask you one other question and then we'll get into creating (or acquiring) your ebook.

Is it possible that you could have identified all the joint venture partners and have written a book that's perfect for your market and still end up with a whole lot of nothing? If so, what would be things that you missed doing that would cause that to happen?

JIM: Once you have researched the demand and made sure you can reach the audience cost-effectively through joint-venture partners, <u>you need to make sure that the target audience is willing to pay for information</u>.

DAVID: **Right.**

JIM: I will share a story with you and this sucks. (Laughter)

Here's where the disappointment can hit you right where you live. And I got sucked in because it was a family member, because I love my dad and because of what seemed like the right reasons, but were the wrong reasons from a business perspective.

On a positive note: this learning experience did help me perfect the last part of the "Ultimate Ebook Success Formula", so the lesson learned is worth many tens-of-thousands of dollars to me!

DAVID: **Okay.**

JIM: Don't get me wrong, we still sell this book and make some money with it, we're just not selling the numbers that we thought we were going to sell.

The book's called "26 Key Typing Tutorial."

DAVID: **Tell me about it.**

JIM: This is an ebook about learning how to type. It was written from a manuscript that my dad came up with 20 years ago where he had two weeks to teach a bunch of people who didn't know how to type how to type at least 30 words a minute… and he did it! He figured out a way to use subconscious programming techniques to teach people to type around 30 words a minute in two weeks or less.

DAVID: **That's pretty cool!**

JIM: I thought it was *really* cool.

Before we converted it to an ebook I went and did some research. I went to keyword tool at **Overture**, at the time it was GoTo, and I looked up how many people were searching for the keywords "typing", "typing tutorial", and related words. I saw there were tens of thousands of people looking for "typing tutorial", "typing coach", all this "typing" related information.

I said to myself, "This is great!"

And then I looked a little further and said, "Man, I can buy these keywords for five, six cents a pop." And that should have been my clue right there. Okay, all those searches—

DAVID: [laughter]

JIM: Yeah, you can laugh now, but that's why it's called a learning experience.

DAVID: Yeah.

JIM: So my dad's all juiced! He's seen how well we've done with these other ebooks and I started telling him about the traffic and what we could do, what we could buy it for... and he's already spending the money, because he *knows* we're going to make it.

He's not literally spending the money, but mentally his eyes are getting big at our prospect. I'll have to admit I was very excited too!

DAVID: Oh, I understand that "wide-eyed" look.

JIM: So I write this sales letter that's really good and we put this thing together. I devoted a lot of time to figuring out how to create a typing tutorial book where people could actually type into the ebook in PDF format. We laid the whole thing out and I invested, I would say I invested 1 1/2 to 2 solid weeks in this thing.

DAVID: Uh-huh.

JIM: And we roll it out and I buy all these top keywords on the pay-per-click search engines, because I didn't have to pay that much for them…

And I ran a thousand people across this website…

… and we sold two. <frown>

DAVID: Not good!

JIM: No. And so I say, "Okay, it's the sales letter, it's the sales letter!" So I redid the sales letter and I ran another thousand people across this website… and we sold one.

And I'm starting to freak out because we've run two thousand people across a website, there's tons of people looking, I've got no trouble getting traffic to this thing and then I decide to go out and take a look and see what these people are buying.

And then I get smacked with a baseball bat right to the face when I realized that they're looking for information, but they're not willing to pay for it…

DAVID: … and all of a sudden you realize, that's why the keywords are so cheap!

JIM: That's why the keywords were so cheap and that's why nobody's buying it, because there's so much stuff out there available for nothing — for free.

DAVID: Yeah.

JIM: Like I said — that was really the final piece of the puzzle for me as far as understanding what it really takes when you do the research and when you're out there looking to survey the market.

You've got to make sure there are people out there who can sell your ebook for you.

You've got to make sure that you can test it cheaply using pay-per-click traffic or ezine ads, but you also got to make sure that even if there's a whole lot of that activity out there that ultimately people are actually willing to pay for the information.

> **HOT TIP**: If people can get everything that you're selling really easily, really cheaply and for free, unless you can put another angle on it that'll make them want to pay for it, then keep going and look for another market.

<u>DON'T take the time to create that ebook</u>!

DAVID: You know, I have a couple of thoughts, and I want to share that what you are saying is brilliant!

The way anyone's ebook is going to succeed is if you can find people who are going to sell it for you, it you can test it cheaply and if the people in the market will spend money for it, that's the key to success in this whole thing with ebooks.

JIM: Right! And if people want a down-and-dirty method for testing out that demand and whether people will pay, then they need to check out the step-by-step bonus for using Overture to research a topic, **BONUS #1 "Best-Selling eBook Topic Detective"**.

In it I will show you not only how to research your topic, but how to predict with a high degree of accuracy whether the market will pay or not.

DAVID: **Oh, boy!**

JIM: It basically shows you how to search around, how to look at competitors and how to gauge market interest.

DAVID: **That's incredible!**

Okay. So let's move now into creating your ebook...

Section 8

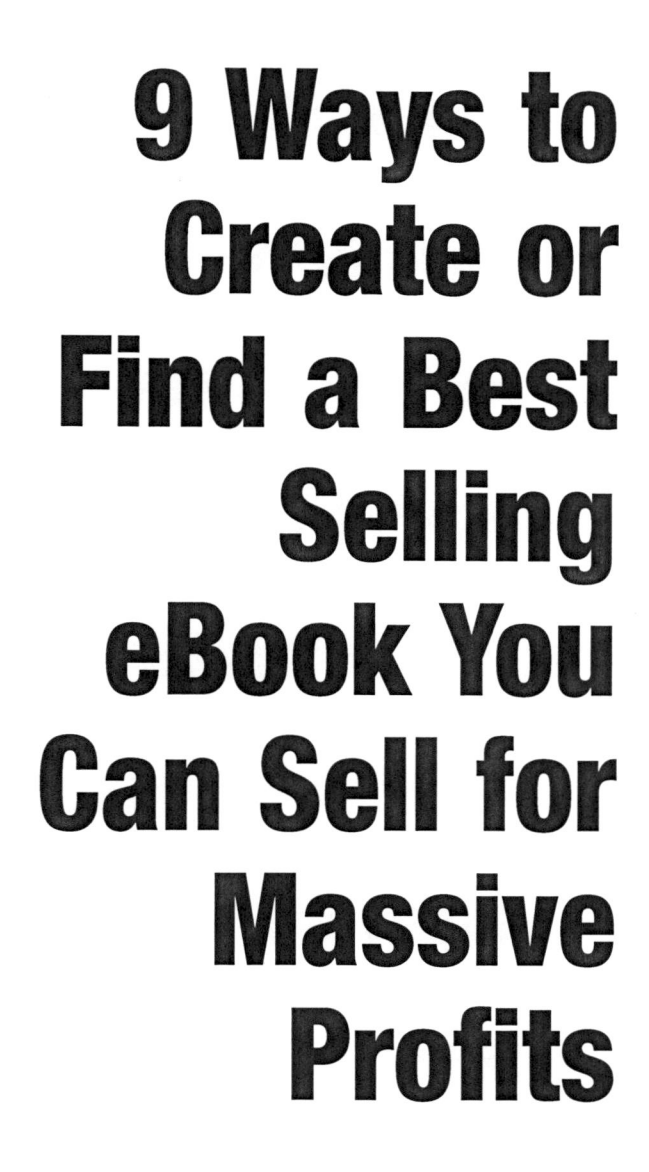

9 Ways to Create or Find a Best Selling eBook You Can Sell for Massive Profits

9 Ways to Create or Find a Best Selling eBook You Can Sell for Massive Profits
SECTION 8

DAVID: So, I want to get in this business. I want to write an ebook to make a lot of money. What in the world am I going to write about?

JIM: What you're going actually going to write about is going to be one of those top ten things or reasons that people buy!

Remember?

1. make money
2. save money
3. save time
4. avoid effort
5. get more comfort
6. achieve greater cleanliness
7. obtain fuller health
8. escape physical pain

9 gain praise

10 to be popular.

That's what you're going to write about. One or some combination of those topics is what you'll write about for your specific niche market.

Here are a couple of examples:

EXAMPLE #1

<u>Niche market</u>: People who want to learn how to write sales copy for their website to convert visitors to sales.

<u>Their Problem</u>: They don't have a lot of time to learn to write copy and they need to produce persuasive, money-making copy quickly.

<u>The Solution</u>: Write an ebook that shows them how to easily write copy (#4 avoid effort), use it to persuade people to buy from their sites (#1 make money) and do it in a way that they can create a winning sales letter in less than two hours (#3 save time).

<u>Potential Title</u>: ***The Quick and Easy Website Copy Writing Guide*** — "Watch your online profits explode with this step-by-step manual for creating professional level website copy results in as little as 2 hours!"

EXAMPLE #2

<u>Niche market</u>: People who want to learn how to make money selling items at online auction sites.

Their Problem: Once they've emptied their garage and attic, they need to know where to find items to "buy low and sell high". They need to know how to accept credit cards. They need to know how to keep from getting ripped off by unscrupulous buyers. They need to know how to make enough sales in a short enough period of time so they can have a life and not be tied to their computer. The need to know how to write their item descriptions and sales pages for maximum bid profit.

The Solution: Write an ebook that shows them all the places buy items for pennies on the dollar and resell them online for huge profits (#1 make money). Show them how to quickly spot a bargain with high resale potential (#2 save money — keep from wasting money). Show them how to find out what the hottest sellers are so they only work in those markets and don't waste time on slow sellers or low margin items (#3 save time). Show them how to use cheap and easy automation tools to automate most of their business so they can concentrate on making money (#4 avoid effort).

Potential Title: *The Online Auction Seller's Bible* — "Learn the secret tips, tricks and techniques the pro's use to create an executive level income using online auctions like eBay."

DAVID: And it's obviously got to be a subject that interests me and that would interest my audience as well.

JIM:	Let me ask you this, David. Why do you go online? When you search the web what are you're looking for?

DAVID:	**Stuff I'm interested in.**

JIM:	Right. You're looking for information you're interested in. More often than not, <u>are you trying to solve a problem</u>?

DAVID:	**Yes. I might be trying to figure out how to get somewhere on an airplane cheaper, or maybe I've been working too hard and I want to take a vacation. So I'm going to start reading about different destinations.**

Another reason I go online is I need to get some information for a project I'm working on… so it's a research thing.

JIM:	Yeah. You're looking to solve a problem. At least for most people, <u>solving a problem is typically a reason to spend money to buy information</u>.

If it's something that's going to help you get away from pain or it's going to help you to gain immediate pleasure, then you're going to be most likely to buy that information rather than to continue to look for it for free… especially if it is very hard to find information.

HOT TIP	The more <u>pressing the need</u>, the more <u>immediate the need</u>, the more <u>intense the pain</u>, or the higher the degree of <u>desire to gain pleasure</u>, the more likely someone is to actually buy your ebook.

So, whatever you write about, the best stuff to write about are ebooks that <u>solve problems</u>, ebooks that <u>alleviate pain</u>, or ebooks that <u>teach skills that make a difference in somebody's</u>

life. If someone believes they can learn a skill that will help them make money, save money, avoid pain and/or get pleasure, they will buy the ebook!

Write an ebook that helps people get more of what they want!

DAVID: **And probably it would be best that people don't think they can easily get this information for free.**

JIM: Exactly. Or, if they can get it for free, but they can't get for free it all in one spot, easily digestible and full of your insider-information.

DAVID: **Okay. That's great. So how do I write my ebook really, really fast?**

JIM: Well, one of the things you need to do is you need to <u>stop thinking of an ebook as a book</u>! Why?

Because as soon as you think of an ebook as a book you limit yourself! Books only have a perceived value of between $10 paperback, up to $30 hardcover. You must stop thinking of it as a book and you must start thinking of it as a neatly packaged solution to a problem.

People aren't buying a book, they are buying a solution — they're buying a result!

And because of that, your ebook doesn't have to be 100, 300, 400 pages long. I've seen some ebooks that have done very well that are only 50 pages long. Now as soon as you start getting down to an ebook that's 10, 20 pages long, unless it is so packed with value and has such a "WOW" factor, when someone pays $30 for only 20 pages worth of information they may get upset that it's only 10-20 pages.

So, I'm going to outline for you now several real fast ways to come up with an ebook… <u>even one you didn't write yourself</u>!

EBOOK CREATION METHOD #1

The first thing you can do, if you know a subject really, really well, is just create an ebook using your knowledge — and you don't even have to write it. You can create it by talking, and then edit a transcript, or hire an editor to do that for you (www.elance.com).

You create an outline of all the points you want to cover and then you use a service like www.idictate.com, which is what we used to create this ebook, or you use a software program called IBM Via Voice, which I got for $29.00 at Staples and you simply just "talk" the ebook out.

The first step is to create an outline of the points you want to cover. Using your organized list of points, you sit there and pretend like you're talking to a friend and explain the subject or solve the problem or give them the information they need to obtain the skill… or whatever you're accomplishing for them in the ebook.

You simply just talk it out and cover each point in as much detail as you can. This works great if you have mastery of a specific subject.

DAVID: **Okay…. That is a great one for consultants, or professionals or really anyone with a specific skill or expertise people are willing to pay for. This is a quick-and-deadly way for people to come up with that $29 calling card we talked about.**

JIM: Exactly!

EBOOK CREATION METHOD #2

If you don't have a specific expertise, then find someone who does, because the next way to come up with your ebook really fast is to do an expert interview format, which is the exact format that we're using here.

David's interviewing me and eliciting the information from my head so that we can convey my knowledge to you. We spent a lot of time, a couple of days in fact, coming up with a list of questions David was going to ask me knowing that he would help guide the interview by interjecting questions as the information started flowing out of me.

So, all you would do is just get on a conference call with your expert and then log on to www.idictate.com, or some other dictation service, and talk it out. When you get the manuscript you would just edit through it for content, add some links, and pretty much you've got the ebook done.

DAVID: An EXCELLENT strategy!

JIM: ## EBOOK CREATION METHOD #3

Another way to get an ebook is simply buy the resale rights to someone else's book, or to cut a marketing deal with them. There are a lot of people out there who've written really good books, but have no clue how to market them.

There are several publishers online who started out publishing their own ebooks and now make a whole lot more money simply marketing ebooks for authors who don't know anything about marketing. But you can also buy the resell rights to a book, such as our "33 Days To Online Profits", and sell it and keep all the money.

There are a few things you need to remember if you are going to buy the resell rights from somebody else:

1. <u>You want to ask how long it's been online</u>. If they won't tell you then you probably just want to move on because that is really a basic question and anyone who won't tell you how long a book has been online probably won't deal with you fairly on other issues.

   A book that has been online for a couple of years might still have a lot of life left in it, but if you see the book everywhere you turn around you might want to keep looking. Trust your gut when it comes to whether you think the market is saturated or not.

2. <u>You want to evaluate the size of the overall niche market it targets</u>. A book that's been on the market for a long time and has a very small niche market may not be the best ebook to invest in resale rights.

   However, an ebook with a huge and recurring market might be a great choice no matter how long it has been online. If lots of new people are coming online who need the information, then you might want to jump on that resale opportunity.

   One surefire way to get a feeling for the size of the market is to go through the process in BONUS#1 — Best-Selling eBook Topic Detective. As you do your research you can see how big the potential market is, how much market penetration the ebook already has (is every other site already selling it?) and how likely it might be that you can engage joint venture partners to work with you.

3. You want to evaluate how good the book is as far as the quality of the information. If the book's really good and you can endorse it to your list or somebody else's list,

then you can easily make your money back and then turn a profit no matter how old the book is.

- Do you like the book?
- Does it contain really good information?
- Is it up-to-date?
- Does it fulfill the promises it makes on the sales letter?
- If you paid for it would you feel like you got your money's worth?
- Will the information stay current for a good while into the future or will you be out of business with it within a couple of months?

These are all questions you need to ask yourself before investing in resale rights for an ebook.

Buying the resale rights to somebody else's book, or creating a marketing deal with somebody else who has an ebook, but no marketing skills, is a great way to get your own ebook to sell.

DAVID: **I like that one — it's fast and simple — just make sure you either have someone to help you sell it or you have your own list to promote it to once you buy the rights!**

JIM: Agreed!

EBOOK CREATION METHOD #4

Another way to get your own ebook to sell is to have someone else do a research project for you on a specific topic. You can hire somebody from www.elance.com — which is basically the "eBay" of freelance people. You could put up a description of a research project that you want somebody to do for you and have people bid on it.

Maybe you want them to find 100 web sites to do something or have them write up step-by-step instructions to accomplish some end result — or whatever it is you want them to do. What you're doing is having them write up big chunks of the book — just don't tell them what it's for.

Make sure you have them do it as what's called a "work for hire", which means that you own the work completely after you pay them.

The research project will cost you anywhere from $100 to several hundred dollars or more, depending on the size of the project. Once your researcher hands over the part(s) of the book they compile, you would add on the introduction, the conclusion and whatever other parts of the book where you were applying your own expertise.

DAVID: **How do you do a "work for hire" agreement?**

JIM: You can find examples of work for hire agreements you can adapt if you do a search on www.google.com for the term "work for hire agreement" or you can ask your attorney to fix you up with a simple one.

DAVID: **I love to use Google to find those types of things.**

JIM: Let me give you an example, of an ebook research project that I might consider hiring somebody to do… and anybody who reads this is free to steal my idea… I can come up with more.

There's a guy who publishes an ebook called "The ebook Writer's Market", and it's kind of a knock-off of a book called "The Writer's Market", which is a directory of publishers of regular books.

What this guy did was he compiled a big list of sites that sell ebooks. For writers who don't know about marketing, ebook authors can get this list and they can take what feels like a more traditional approach to marketing their book. They can list their book with these "bookstores" or book publishers and he's got all these different ones cataloged in his ebook.

The problem is the information in the book goes out of date really fast because these ebook selling sites come and go and they're not cataloged very well. He's got them listed alphabetically if I'm not mistaken.

A better way to do this would be to (and it could be a valuable service) have somebody research all of these sites and come up with a classification system. Then have the sites entered into a simple database that could be searched online. Then you would have a database that people could buy a membership to and they could come and do an initial search to find publishers, ebook stores, and other places where they could list their ebook for sale.

They could then come back and check on a periodic basis for additional publishers and bookstores to sell their ebook as they come online.

I would hire someone to do the initial research, then hire somebody else to set up the database and then sell it as a service that they pay $40 — 50 to join and then whatever the market tells me I could charge on a monthly or yearly recurring basis to stay a member. And then I would simply just pay somebody on an hourly basis every month to update the links and to look for new places that these authors could post their ebooks for sale.

If someone does take this idea, all I ask is you give me a free membership.

DAVID: **It sounds like a great idea. There are enough people who are interested in this topic, in writing ebooks right now, so it could be a valuable business.**

JIM: Sure, or another way to use a research project is if you wanted to publish an ebook on the 50 best sites to accomplish some objective, such as the 50 best travel sites.

Or, if you wanted to publish a step-by-step guide, you could have somebody who understood how to do something step-by-step — for example how to install a CGI script on your website — write up the steps for you in plain language. You would then just dress their instructions up a bit and, presto, virtually an instant ebook with a step-by-step solution to somebody's problem.

> **HOT TIP**
>
> See, you don't have to know how to install CGI scripts on a website to sell a book about how to install CGI scripts! You just hire somebody that knows how to do it, suck the information out of their head by having them either write it up or by interviewing them, you buy that from them as a "work for hire" and then you go sell it!

DAVID: Cool!

JIM: **EBOOK CREATION METHOD #5**

Another way would be to do a small seminar in front of a group of people, record it, and have it transcribed. Doing a seminar in front of a small bunch of people is a great way to get audience feedback, audience reaction and, by responding to their questions, it will really draw the good points out of you that you may not have considered before.

And, you can get paid for creating your ebook this way by charging an admission fee to the seminar!

This is good if you really understand a specific topic well and don't mind speaking in public.

DAVID: What else?

JIM:

EBOOK CREATION METHOD #6

Another way is to do a teleconference. It's the same thing as doing a seminar in front of a group of people except that everybody's on the telephone. One of the great things about doing that is the services usually record it for you and can have it transcribed so you end up with several different products that you can sell: a tape, a CD and an ebook (transcript).

One service I know you've used, David, is www.voicetext.com.

EBOOK CREATION METHOD #7

Another way to come up with an ebook really fast is to find a book or a government report that's in the public domain. Now, public domain means that it's free to be published by anybody, and many government reports are in the public domain.

You can sell these reports if they are in the public domain — though you may want to add to them and spice them up with links, articles and other things you can use to make them even more valuable.

You can get a lot of information about how public domain works and related subjects just by going to www.google.com or www.yahoo.com and put in "public domain information" and go from there. The most critical issue about selling documents in the public domain is verifying that they are, in fact, in the public domain.

Most books written before 1922 are mostly in the public domain and you need to check this out. One of the bonuses with this ebook is a common sense guide to understanding copyright that we actually got from the copyright office — so it's straight from the horse's mouth!

Here are a few online resources to help get you started:

- http://www.bf.org/copylaw.htm
- http://www.unc.edu/~unclng/public-d.htm
- http://www.savetz.com/pd/

[Please note that we take no responsibility for the content on these pages. We are not providing legal advice. Only information. It is your responsibility to verify whether a work is truly in the public domain.]

This little-known method for turning out an ebook is the reason why you see a lot of people advertising these "lost manuscripts" they've discovered.

I've got a book right here that was copyrighted in 1918 so it's in the public domain. It's called "114 Proved Plans to Save a Busy Man Time." Now do you think the principals of time management have really changed a whole lot between now and close to a hundred years ago?

DAVID: **Probably not.**

JIM: The answer is no — the principles of time management have not changed!

So this book is divided into over a hundred different little one to two page snippets that show you how to save time with your work. Now, don't you think that I can take 15, 20 or 30 of these snippets, adapt them and turn then into a newsletter that I can deliver automatically to people who either do or don't buy the Lazy Man's Guide to Online Business? Of course!

I can start building this huge list of people that are interested in getting more done faster for less money... and someone else has done the hard work of creating the content.

DAVID: **Oh, that's really good. So, what you did is you carved it up into little tips which you're sending out on a list and you're updating and rewriting it in case someone renewed the copyright.**

JIM: Absolutely.

But if it's in the public domain you don't have to even rewrite it. You should really take the time to find out more about public domain and how you can get started this way. Again, I can't give legal advice here, but a quick search for "public domain" in www.google.com will get you started.

DAVID: **Oh, that's fabulous. I see. That's very creative... and now you've got two years worth of newsletters.**

JIM: Absolutely!

DAVID: **So how did you find that book?**

JIM: I found it at a site called www.alibris.com and actually I didn't find it. My buddy Yanik Silver found it and emailed it to me... and told me that I owed him big time.

DAVID: **(Laughter). Okay. That's great.**

JIM: So, that's why you see these "lost" manuscripts that people are selling because you can sell somebody else's book that's already written and keep all the profits. They're not lost — they are just re-purposed in a new era.

DAVID: Yep.

JIM: **EBOOK CREATION METHOD #8**

Another way, and we touched on this sort of when I said earlier that if you could find somebody who's got an ebook done, but they don't have any marketing skills. The other way is simply to find an author who really doesn't have any marketing skills, but who has one heck of an expertise and is very hungry to make money.

Then what you do is you help them write a book either by interviewing them or by writing the sales letter ahead of time and saying, "Hey, this sales letter is great, now write the book that fulfills all the promises I made in this sales letter."

DAVID: **Sure. Oh I like that one.... So you create the "wish" list in the sales letter and someone else creates the product and you sell it.**

JIM: Which is definitely a proven step in the process of creating an ebook that absolutely rocks! You could either pay the author a flat fee for rights to the book, a percentage of sales or make some other financial arrangement.

The guy that I mentioned before who has that stop your divorce website, his name is Dean Jackson, but he didn't write that book. He tells a story about how he found a guy who did counseling who was advertising in USA Today trying to sell a book through a little classified ad.

DAVID: Ah.

JIM: He called the guy up and the ultimate deal that he cut with him was that he gets all the money from the sale of the ebook and the counselor gets all of the backend counseling that comes out of him having published the book.

DAVID: **Okay.**

JIM: So, Dean wrote the sales letter, he interviewed the guy, he found all the hot buttons that people would be interested in who are having that particular difficulty with their marriage, and solved all the major problems they have with the way that he interviewed this counselor to create the ebook.

DAVID: **I see.**

JIM: He found somebody who had the expertise, who had the skills, who had the knowledge and simply sucked it out of his head.

DAVID: **How's the counselor doing, is he getting a lot of calls?**

JIM: Apparently he gets a ton of calls and gets a ton of business out of it.

DAVID: **And is he making a lot of money?**

JIM: I don't know. He makes it very obvious both on the sales letter and in the ebook that you can and should call him for an individualized counseling session.

I have to believe that if they're selling thirty to thirty-five thousand dollars worth a month at $79 a pop like Dean says they are, then a certain percentage of those people have got to be contacting this guy for counseling.

You can check out their site at **http://www.eBookSecretsExposed.com/syd.html**

DAVID: **Yeah, that's really good! Any other ways to write an ebook fast?**

JIM: **EBOOK CREATION METHOD #9**

One of the ways that a lot people use to create an ebook is interviewing a bunch of experts on a certain subject and compiling it into an ebook.

DAVID: **I've been interviewed for several of those. I think you have too, Jim.**

JIM: Yes, but one mistake some of those people make is that they just have raw interviews in their ebook.

They don't really edit the interviews, they don't really take the time to develop the questions and to elicit the best answers from these people.

Typically what they do is just send a list of questions via email. The people they're interviewing, especially the more desirable ones, don't have much time to give to the answers.

As a result, they just rattle off a few answers and then these "authors" compile those answers <u>unedited</u> into an ebook and expect the thing to sell, but it's usually a piece of crap!

So if you're going to do interviews, you better get real good, meaty interviews that explain a specific topic or an area of a topic in good detail, otherwise, don't bother.

DAVID: Okay. Fair enough. So when I create my ebook, how do I make it such that it's practically guaranteed that <u>other people</u> will want to sell if <u>for me</u>?

JIM: You have to create your ebook in a way that totally meets the needs of their audience with a price point that will make it a no-brainer for them to buy!

But the way to do it is to make sure that you create it with the needs and wants of that audience totally in mind. Not writing what <u>you</u> want to write, but writing what <u>they want</u> and are <u>willing to pay</u> for in mind.

If you have researched your audience correctly, you should have a really good idea of what their problems are. If you don't, then you need to look at the publications they read and see what types of topics are featured.

- What problems do those articles address or solve?
- What are some recurring themes they deal with?
- What questions or issues do you see people discussing in the online forums where your target audience congregates? Are these issues you can address?

Once you have made this determination, then you need to speak directly to their wants and desires by use their language to express the topic of your ebook.

Here are a couple of examples:

If your audience needs help installing CGI scripts, your title could be "How to Quickly and Easily Install CGI Scripts — for Non-Technical People" and the topic is all about how people with average computer skills can learn to install CGI scripts in a couple of hours.

*** Don't try to turn them into computer programmers or give them the history or CGI scripting — just give them a quick and dirty guide, a "survival" guide to installing the scripts themselves.

If your audience wants to learn how to quit smoking, your title could be "Quit Smoking Once And For All — Right Now!" and the topic is all about how to quickly stop smoking with the least amount of withdrawal symptoms, mood swings or other negative side effects.

*** Don't try to give them a lecture or a medical explanation! Give them techniques and strategies that work to help them make it through tomorrow — and beyond — without starting smoking again.

DAVID: **Can you give me an example of a way to approach something where the audience won't be interested in it and a way to approach the same subject where they would be very interested in it? A specific example?**

JIM: Sure, here's a real world example.

When I wrote "The Lazy Man's Guide to Online Business", I co-wrote that with my dad and originally the name of that book was "How to Get More Done Faster". I thought that was a great title, but unfortunately, a lot of other people didn't think that was a hot title because "getting more done faster" sounds like we're going to teach you how to do a whole lot more in a lot less time and it's just going to be a big pain in the butt.

I was not paying attention to what the audience was looking for.

But then we realized that what people were trying to do — and what we really were teaching people — was how to actually do less and make more for the effort they put out and, in the end, enjoy themselves and their life a lot more. So we ended up changing the name to "The Lazy Man's Guide to Online Business — How to Work Less, Get Paid More and Have Tons More Fun" and as soon as we did that, sales started taking off like a rocket.

DAVID: **That's a great example. Now, did you change the contents of the book at all?**

JIM: No. I didn't change the content except where I had to change the reference to the title in the book itself and I tweaked it a little bit. Other than that it is the exact same book.

DAVID: **Okay. That's a great example because it's such a minor adjustment but you must have seen multiples in the effectiveness of your copy and the sales result.**

JIM: Oh, it was the difference between night and day. It was just totally different as soon as we changed that title. As soon as we made those little changes in the book, I started having people showing up, knocking on my door and asking me if they could sell it for me.

We increased our results tremendously just from focusing exclusively on what my <u>audience wanted</u> and <u>communicating it in terms that were important to them</u> — not communicating in terms that were important to me!

Speaking their language was the final key to the success of that project!

Section 9

How Can I Use an eBook To Get More Consulting or Coaching Business

How Can I Use an eBook To Get More Consulting or Coaching Business

SECTION 9

DAVID: Now, another question. You were talking about that guy, Homer McDonald, the marriage therapist in Texas, the stop your divorce guy.

http://www.eBookSecretsExposed.com/syd.html

How does someone use an ebook to do what he did — that is, to draw people who want to hire him to consult, speak, to do coaching, counseling or therapy over the phone for big bucks?

How can someone use an ebook to get people to buy more of their products and services? In other words, how do people use their ebook as a way to attract customers to buy their other stuff where they make even more money?

JIM: If what you're asking is how do you write an ebook to get people to buy more of your personal services or more of your expertise type products…

DAVID: Exactly.

JIM: …then what you have to do is write an ebook that proves, in the mind of your prospect, that you are the expert in your field.

DAVID: **Okay.**

JIM: By proving you are the expert, you have to solve somebody's problem based on your own personal experience, your own work experience, your own past experience and what you have to offer as a result of whatever services your provide.

So, a real estate agent might write a book on how to sell your house yourself (and in my case I did).

In the sales letter where I sell the ebook, I talk about my qualifications and credentials as part of the sales pitch to "prove" that I should know what I'm talking about…

When I was actively selling real estate in my local market, I had a full page in the book that had a mini-resume on it, told about how I did things better, different and more effectively than other agents. It also had a very obvious call to action at the bottom of the page that told them if they needed help in my market area that they should call me, email me, fax me or do whatever to get into contact with me.

By selling and using this ebook in my local market (I also had neatly bound copies done up at Kwik Kopy to hand out), I used it as my $29 calling card. Anytime I came across someone who could potentially hire me if they ended up not selling on their own, I just gave them a copy of the book.

I generated an EXTRA $50,000 in commissions the first year I used this strategy.

One of the things I learned is that you should always describe your qualifications in a way that clearly expresses the benefit for the potential purchaser of your services.

For example, most real estate agents have various initials and designations after their names. You've seen them, "GRI",

"CRS", "ABR", "SRES", "President's Club". Nobody knows what those designations mean.

They need to tell people. "I have earned the 'ABR' designation, which means I have been specially trained to help you negotiate the best price, at the best terms, on your next house. My skills mean you won't pay one single dollar more than you have to for your next house... and in today's real estate market it's important for you to have a trained, experience professional who can help you save money!"

The agents who describe how those designations benefit for the consumer do much better. The reason I was able to list so many houses was because I proved I was the expert in the ebook <u>AND</u> I clearly told people how my skills could benefit them in terms they could readily understand.

Because of the way I explained the benefits of working with me, should they not sell on their own for whatever reason, they called me instead of the other 400 agents who didn't have an ebook and who didn't explain their services in terms that related directly to the needs of the customer.

Most of your competition never does that! They're too busy beating the gong saying "Look at me" instead of saying "This is how I can help you".

DAVID: **Oh, that's interesting.**

JIM: So an accountant might write a book on the top 15 ways a corporation can save money on next year's taxes and then a sub headline for that might be "15 legal deductions the IRS has to let you take but they hate every minute of it."

DAVID: **Yeah. They're a great type of ebook to turn out. Very good!**

JIM: Or a chiropractor might do an ebook on nine things you can do to alleviate back pain within 15 minutes and a sub-headline to that might be "what anyone who sits in front of a computer for more than three hours a day should know to avoid back spasms."

DAVID: **I get the picture.**

JIM: But what it does is it targets a niche audience. It targets a niche audience's specific problem and then shows how you are the expert in solving that problem. And by the way, nobody ever just has one problem, they have multiple problems!

So, once you solve that problem they bought the ebook for, then you let them know in a very overt and obvious way, "Hey, my name's Jim Edwards and I'm available to consult with you on your ebook for $1,000 an hour."

DAVID: **Okay.**

JIM: Or, "My name is Dr. Barney Jones and I'm available to consult with your or adjust your back at $75 per session, (whatever it is) and here's a coupon for the first session at 50 percent off."

DAVID: **Right!**

JIM: So you use the ebook literally as a $29 "calling card". Another way you can use it is let's say you've got a prospect for your consulting practice whom you developed through other means, let's say through a newspaper ad. As a way to help cement the relationship and prove you are an expert, you can say to them "Hey, I'll send you a copy of my book" and you email them a copy of your ebook.

Let's say you end up making a $500 sale by giving away what is perceived as a $30 book — which in actuality is just a bunch of bits and bites that don't cost you anything other than the bandwidth to email it so somebody.

So that's another way to use an ebook to make money. It turns into your own personal billboard that demonstrates you have the necessary expertise and tells people they can contact you for more information or for personal services. It gives you a very powerful tool that you can put in the hands of potential consulting customers you develop through other means.

Section 10

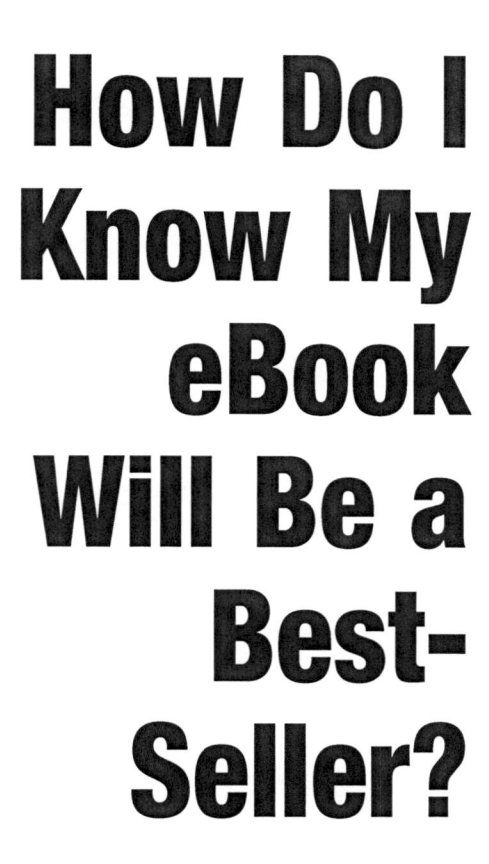

How Do I Know My eBook Will Be a Best-Seller?

How Do I Know My eBook Will Be a Best-Seller?
SECTION 10

DAVID: **In terms of actually making money from selling the ebook itself, how can I know my ebook will be a bestseller before I even create it?**

JIM: Okay. Remember, the first step is that you research to see if there are people out there already selling to your market. You also use the Overture "keyword" tool to see what kind of searches are going on for the specific keywords your people are interested in.

[You should refer to Bonus #1 that we've created on how to do that research step-by-step.]

We talked earlier about how to research and where to look for sites to do potential joint ventures with, but when you look at someone's website, <u>what should you be looking for</u>?

Here are some guidelines when evaluating other people's sites:

- Do they sell other people's products? If they have a bunch of other people's products visibly for sale then that's a great indication they may work with you in the future when you are ready.

- If you can't see they are selling other people's products (especially if it's a one page website), do they appear to be collecting names and emails? If so, that means they have a list they probably mail to that you could potentially hitch a ride on. Sign up for their newsletter or "mini-course" to see what they send out

- Is the site professional looking? It doesn't need to have "flash" and all that other stuff, but do they have their own domain name and does it look like some time, effort and energy went into creating the site. Sites hosted on "geo cities" or some other obviously free and advertising supported service do not usually make great joint venture partners.

- Do you see other people in the same market endorsing someone else's products or ebooks? As you research your market, you will see that certain people get talked about by most or all the rest of the people in the market. Those are the people you want to research and get to know their work. Those are the people who can either help you directly or introduce you to the people who will work with you directly.

Once you've done that research, you should have a pretty good idea that your ebook is going to be a best seller. But, in my opinion, the best way to research is to <u>survey</u> your target audience first…

DAVID: **Okay.**

JIM: … and I explain how to do an actual survey in the included a Special Report "How To Use Simple Surveys to Write a Best Selling eBook" as a bonus to this book.

The one thing I will say about this survey technique is that it works best if you already have a list of your own, but you can also persuade other people to survey their lists and then you can share in the results. Most people don't know how to do surveys, or don't have the time, so if you can show them the benefits to them of doing a survey, they will work with you to gather that marketing intelligence.

You can also post surveys in forums and discussion groups, so it is <u>not required</u> that you have your own list, but it is quicker if you do. I talk about this whole survey process in-depth in BONUS #5: "How to Use Simple Surveys to Write Best-Selling eBooks & Info-Products".

Man we've got enough bonuses, don't we?

DAVID: **Yeah, we do. <smile>**

JIM: In the bonus I show a couple of surveys that I've done and the upshot is that you ask a whole lot of people in your target audience what problems they have, what they're interested in learning how to do, what they want to know more about, what types of things they would be likely to buy within the next six months. Then you simply ask two, three, four, five hundred of them the questions and whatever they answer is what you provide in your ebook!

DAVID: **That's pretty good. So you're not using your intuition or some indirect read of the market place. You're not counting headlines in magazines. You're actually asking the people who might buy it what they want.**

JIM: <u>Exactly</u>. You're <u>asking</u> the people who will buy it what they want and then you just give it to them — that's the way to create a best-seller with the least amount of risk.

In fact, in that bonus about surveys I explain how to increase your response rate dramatically by bribing people to respond and I tell you what kind of questions that you should ask. Basically you should just use a common sense approach and ask people what they bought in the past, what they're likely to buy in the future, and how likely they are to make the actual purchase.

Especially look for what they're most interest in learning "how to do", the problems they're looking to solve, or what pain they're currently feeling. Ask them what they'd be likely to buy in the next six months and then you give them a <u>bribe</u> to answer the survey. You give them a reward for answering your survey.

DAVID: **And do you spell that out, what kind of bribe and so forth?**

JIM: You make it totally obvious. In fact, the surveys that I run, I tell them, "I've got a bribe here for you if you take two minutes to do this survey!" One of my headlines is even "60 Seconds Plus Free Gift".

HOT TIP

And the other thing is you want to make sure your surveys are really short, no more than about five, six, seven questions.

DAVID: **What kinds of things to you bribe them with?**

JIM: One time it was with a free ebook that somebody else wrote, I didn't even write it. It was somebody else's ebook.

This project was done in conjunction with the "33 Days to Online Profits" audience. We wanted to survey them to see what types of products they were most interested in buying in the futures. We wanted to know also what they didn't like about the 33 Days ebook so we could make future products even better.

We came up with a survey they could answer quickly and it had what appeared to be a very valuable bribe for taking the survey.

Here's the actual letter we sent out....

> [[firstname]] — 60 second survey + Free Gift
>
> A Free Gift in return for your help!
>
> Hi [[firstname]]
>
> Jim Edwards from www.33Daystoonlineprofits.com here.
>
> Yanik Silver and I are working on a new project to update and improve the 33 Days to Online Profits program... really take it to the "next level"!
>
> Rather than guess what people want, we decided to ask you - someone who has read the 33 Days program and can give us valuable feedback on how to make it even better!.
>
> ==> A FREE Gift (bribe) for you!
>
> Click this link to take a short survey — it should only take you about 60 seconds (or less) to complete.
>
> ==> http://www.33daystoonlineprofits.com/survey33.html
>
> As a thank you (*bribe*) for filling out the survey we will give you a FREE Gift — a brand NEW ebook by online guru Audri Lanford. She has just realeased a new ebook and Yanik twisted her arm to let us offer this ebook to our 33 Days subscribers for FREE... for a limited time!
>
> (You will *love* this one!)
>
> This ebook has a REAL $29 VALUE!

But it's yours FREE...

"43 Specific Ways to Make 2002 Your Best, Most Profitable Year Ever"

Imagine having 43 of the most successful business leaders, innovators, and experts share with you their best advice on how to make this year your most profitable, successful year ever.

These amazing achievers include:
Jay Abraham
Ken Blanchard
Jim Daniels
Declan Dunn
Allan Gardyne
David Garfinkel   (We know this guy)
John Harricharan
Paul Hartunian
Jonathan Mizel
Joe Vitale
... and Yanik Silver!

Once you complete the survey you will instantly be emailed the information for where to go to download the ebook... you will also be told how to get the ebook with a pop-up window that appears right after you complete the survey.

Please take *60 seconds right now* to fill out the survey and you'll get an INCREDIBLE BONUS for your time!

Click Here to go to the survey

==> http://www.33daystoonlineprofits.com/survey33.html

> Thanks in advance for your feedback and help :-)
>
> Jim Edwards
>
> Co-author "33 Days to Online Profits"
>
> http://www.33daystoonlineprofits.com
>
> =======================
>
> *This email is never sent unsolicited.*
>
> You (or someone with your email address) subscribed at the www.33daystoonlineprofits.com site. If you wish to stop receiving emails from us please see simple removal instructions below.

We ended up having over a 25% response rate to this survey in less than 48 hours! We had more than enough marketing intelligence to create what we believe will be another best-selling info-product. That survey was worth it's weight in gold!

On another survey that I do to the people who purchase "How to Write and Publish Your Own eBook… in as Little as 7 Days", I have the pitch for the survey and the survey all in one email. I inserted that survey into the autoresponder follow-up so now everyone who buys the book gets the survey 37 days after they purchase.

This is a perfect situation for someone who doesn't have a list yet, but does have people signing up for an autoresponder sequence — such as your mini-course. You can make a survey part of your mini-course and give people a bonus with high perceived value in exchange for taking your survey.

Here's the survey I send out to those people who purchase. Please notice how much space and effort I put into explaining the reward they will get for participating…

A Free Gift in return for your help!

Hi [[firstname]]

Jim Edwards from www.7dayebook.com here.

I'm working on a new project that should take ebook writing and marketing to the "next level".

Rather than guess what people want, I decided to ask you - someone who is interested in writing, publishing and selling ebooks.

==> A FREE Gift (bribe) for you!

Below is a short survey — it should only take you about 2 minutes to complete and email back.

As a thank you (*bribe*) for filling out the survey I will send you a FREE Gift — two interviews I did with two of today's top Internet Marketers: Yanik Silver and Danny Sullivan.

(You will *love* this one!)

Yanik Silver talks about how he got started with his Ultra-successful Instant Sales Letters website and how he went from zero (0) to over $100,000 a year in less than 12 months!

Danny Sullivan — the original search engine guru — drops some great nuggets of wisdom about using search engines to promote your site!

You sure won't find these interviews anywhere else on the web for free!

Once you return the survey I will send you the articles personally (since I won't be sending them by autoresponder it may take an hour or two in between checking my mail... but I *will* send them to you)

Please take *two minutes right now* to fill out the survey and you'll get a couple of very informative articles for your time.

Thanks in advance for your feedback and help.

Jim Edwards

Co-author "How to Write and Publish your own eBook... in as little as 7 Days"

http://www.7dayebook.com

=======================

Ebook survey

Directions: Just hit your email "reply button" make "X" marks in between the [ ], fill in numbers, or answer Yes or No as indicated in each question.

Then "send" the survey back to us.

1. Please rank these in order of importance (1,2,3,4,5) with #1 most important, #2 next most important, etc.

[ ] Learning how to get more prospects to your website (traffic)

[ ] Learning how to make more money from each book sale

[ ] Learning about systems / software for ebook delivery

[ ] Learning how to create a stream of "passive" income

[ ] Learning advanced techniques for how to create ebooks quickly

2. Which would you be most likely to buy in the next 6 months (X in each box that applies)

[ ] Ebook "compiler" software (makes "ebooks")

[ ] Advice on Ebook marketing

[ ] Advice on pricing ebooks

[ ] Advanced techniques for selling more ebooks

[ ] Advanced techniques for creating ebooks quickly

[ ] Other: (fill in here)

3. Ebook software

Would you be interested in Independent Reviews of various ebook software creation programs.

[ ] (Yes / No in the box)

If "yes" — How interested? (X in the box)

[ ] Very Interested

[ ] Interested

[ ] Slightly Interested

4. Ebook delivery

Would you be interested in step-by-step, "paint-by-numbers" instruction on how to set up a totally automated ebook delivery system on the web?

[ ] (Yes / No in the box)

If "yes" — How interested? (X in the box)

[ ] Very Interested

[ ] Interested

[ ] Slightly Interested

Thanks for your input. Please email this survey form back along with your name and email to:

Jim Edwards at

info@7dayebook.com

I will send you your FREE gift for taking the time to fill out the survey.

Jim.

http://www.7dayebook.com

=======================

This email is never sent unsolicited.

You (or someone with your email address) subscribed at the www.7dayebook.com site. If you wish to stop receiving emails from us please see below.

Survey results are an excellent way to get information you can use to write or create a best-selling ebook. A free article or ebook is certainly worth two minutes of someone's time and it will increase your response rates incredibly!

Section 11

Publishing Your eBook For The Web

Publishing Your eBook For The Web
SECTION 11

DAVID: **Okay, let's talk about distributing your ebook. How should I publish my book for online distribution? What are my options and why would I choose one over the other?**

JIM: You basically have three options for publishing your ebook online. The first is PDF, which is read with the free program, Adobe Acrobat Reader. PDF stands for "Portable Document Format" and that's my favorite way to deliver an ebook. I'll tell you why in just a minute.

The second option is using a password protected site where your ebook is really a bunch of html pages that people have to pay to get access to.

The third option to distribute your ebook online is to use an html ebook compiler, which creates those ebooks you get that are .exe files. When you click on the .exe ebook files they open up and look like long web pages with very simplistic web browser controls.

My favorite of the three is the PDF format.

DAVID: **Why?**

JIM: It's a long answer. Let's talk about "how" first.

DAVID: **Fair enough. How do you create a PDF?**

JIM: ## METHOD #1 – USING PDF

Well, a PDF is created one of two ways. The first way you can create a basic PDF document (basic means it doesn't have any links in it) is using a free service on www.adobe.com. This service, which lets you create your PDF document for free, will convert a Word file or a Corel WordPerfect file into PDF for you over the Internet.

Here's the link → **https://createpdf.adobe.com**

A note of caution that this service doesn't convert web-links from your word processor document. It does, however, create a very nice basic PDF file.

You can buy the full version of Adobe Acrobat, which costs between $200 and $250 bucks retail, though you can check on eBay (the online auction super site) and probably find it for cheaper. I just this minute searched eBay and found version 5.0 (the most current version as of this writing) up for bid at $149.

If you know a student who can go into a college bookstore and buy an academic version, they can get it for a lot cheaper. I got mine for $99 that way.

Also, you can check on Amazon.com and see if they are running any specials. I saw it on there one time with a $60 rebate and some other offers that made the final price $166.

Regardless of how you get it, any serious online ebook and info-publisher should have the full version.

The reason that I love PDF is that it's very stable and it's virtually virus-proof. Any time you send somebody a .exe file or some sort of executable file, there's potential for that file to become corrupt or to be infected with a virus… while PDF documents are virtually virus-proof.

This means you don't have to worry about spreading a virus with your ebook, which is very important because that is a surefire way to lose customers. Send them a virus after they have paid you money and they will no longer be a customer.

DAVID: **That's fairly certain.**

JIM: The other great thing about PDFs is that you can embed hidden links in them. So, remember we've been talking about setting up a backend income stream using your affiliate links? Well, you can format your links so it says "Visit Bob's Web site", **click here**, and underneath that, it's linked to your affiliate link... but they can't really see that they're clicking on an actual affiliate link.

DAVID: **Very clever.**

JIM: So it's kind of like a little "Trojan Horse" in your ebook.

DAVID: **That's great!**

JIM: And the other great thing about PDFs is that you can control the exact look and feel of your document. No matter what computer they're looking at it on, no matter what size monitor they have, no matter what colors, no matter all that stuff, you can control exactly the look and feel of the page the information shows up on.

You can have a little masthead at the top, you can have your page numbers at the bottom, you can have your copyright notice on every single page, you can format it however you want, and when you're done formatting it and convert it to PDF, that's exactly how it's going to look.

You can also enjoy a much better level of security with a PDF because you can save your PDF so that nobody can change it, so that nobody can even copy and paste the text out of it if you want to.

You can even password protect the PDF so people need a password to open it, though I don't ever really do that. You could if you wanted to, though people can just give the password. So there's a lot better security and the files are often smaller than those .exe ebook compilers.

DAVID: **So a PDF will download faster?**

JIM: Yes. It will usually download faster, not always, but most of the time.

DAVID: **Okay.**

JIM: And a PDF document works on virtually any computer on any operating system that can connect to the Internet. So if they're using a PC or if they're using a Macintosh, it doesn't matter. They can read and view your ebook, and by the way, those .exe ebook compilers <u>don't work on a Macintosh</u>.

DAVID: **Okay.**

JIM: The upshot with PDF, what this means to you, is that if you can type into a word processor and make it look the way you want it to look, then you can convert it to PDF and that's exactly how the ebook is going to look.

DAVID: **So it doesn't take a whole lot of learning of new skills?**

JIM: No, it behaves virtually just like using a printer.

DAVID: **Okay, that's good. What about the other options for publishing?**

JIM: **METHOD #2 – USING A "PASSWORD PROTECTED SITE"**

With a password protected site that contains a bunch of html pages that deliver your information, the advantage is that it's <u>easy to update</u>.

With a PDF document, once you put it up there on the web and start selling it, you can't really go out and edit the thousand ebooks you've already sold.

DAVID: **That's true.**

JIM: Whereas with a password protected site, you can update one page and everybody who logs in to look at it can instantly get the updated information. You update everyone all at once because they are all looking at the same copy of the information.

This is the best publishing method for information that's going to change frequently. Remember the example I gave with the idea about the ebook writers' market with all those ebook related web sites?

DAVID: **Yeah.**

JIM: That would be a perfect application for this, in fact, any type of collection of sites. There's another publication out there called "Directory of Ezines" (formerly known as "Lifestyles Pub"), They're at http://www.ebooksecretsexposed.com/ezinedir.html

DAVID: **Okay. What do they do?**

JIM: They sell a yearly membership to a site that classifies and categorizes ezines, those thousands of email newsletters that populate the web. So whether you want to distribute free articles, you want to distribute content or you want to buy ads or look for joint venture partners... you just enter in certain criteria, click a button and it gives you a list of all the ezines that match that criteria.

<u>This service saves you hours and hours of searching</u> through other listing services that are free, but a lot less organized. That's how these guys make money — just by making life easier for you. So that's another example of an information product that is hidden behind a password protected area.

And though you can control access to a point, you can't really keep people from sharing their username and password.

And there are some disadvantages that come along with hiding your ebook as html pages behind a password protected area.

Number one, it's a heck of a lot more complicated to set up. You've got a lot more systems that you have to hope keep working and, if you're a non-technical person like me, if something breaks, you usually freak out because you have no clue how to fix it or how long it will be down.

DAVID: **Oh yeah. Been there, done that!**

JIM: Then you ask why it's down? Or, how much will the person you hired to help you charge you to make it work again? My favorite technical support questions is, "Why did it stop working in the first place and why do I have to pay this person to fix something that shouldn't have broken in the first place?"

DAVID: **Yeah. I've always wondered that too! <smile>**

JIM: Another problem with having password protected sites is that people lose their passwords. So you create another stream of work for yourself (or you have to pay somebody) to help people sort things out when they've lost their password.

And I know that you can buy programs that will automatically email people their password, except that there are a lot of people who forget the email address they used when they registered... or can't remember what their username was so that you can email them their password.

Another frequent complaint that I get from people when they talk about authors who publish using html pages on a password protected site is that most people who buy your ebook are going to print off all or part of the ebook so that they can read it offline and make notes on the paper.

With an html page, or a series of html pages, it's very hard for them to print it off and put it into a three-ring binder because none of the pages have numbers on them. The same goes for those ebook compilers too!

DAVID: **Yeah, that is a problem.**

JIM: Since people can't easily print those html pages off and you're trying to sell it as an ebook, you will tend to frustrate people in many cases.

However, despite the drawbacks, this is a valid way to sell an info-product if it makes sense and if you can't do it as a PDF.

METHOD #3 – USING AN "EBOOK COMPILER"

The third way to publish is with the html ebook compiler, which I think you can tell so far I'm not a big fan of. One of the many reasons I'm not a big fan of those is that people can more easily access your ebook's "source files".

In the cheaper compilers I have see, that means somebody could get into your text and really just slurp it out and start manipulating it in order to rip off or alter your ebook. Some of the more expensive compilers have safeguards against that, but, again, they're not compatible with Macs!

What you need to keep in mind is that Macs are usually owned by very passionate people. They're very defensive about the fact that they have a Mac and people make things they cannot use, such as ebooks that use .exe files.

DAVID: **Yup.**

JIM: And if you cut them out of your niche audience by making it impossible for them to read and use your ebook, they'll be pretty vocal about it.

DAVID: **Yes. They will <grin>**

JIM: And I will say this about the people who own Macs: typically I've found them to be very Internet savvy and extremely computer literate and you want to make your information available to that audience… because they are buyers!

DAVID: **I agree.**

JIM: So, you know, another gripe I have with html ebook compilers is that it's really a lot harder to control the look and feel of the ebook… which is important because you want to have a nice, organized presentation.

DAVID: **Yes. When it's your ebook, you want to be in control.**

JIM: So what that means to you is that it's going to cost you a little bit of money to buy the Adobe Acrobat program, the full version of the program, and learn how to use it.

If you don't want to do that, then get your ebook completely formatted in Microsoft Word or Corel WordPerfect and then you can hire somebody from Elance to convert your document to PDF for you for probably 20 to 40 bucks.

http://www.eBookSecretsExposed.com/elance.html

DAVID: **Any advice about formatting?**

JIM: Regarding PDF's — here's one that cost me, cost me big time, because I learned this one the hard way.

HOT TIP
If you are using Adobe Acrobat 5.0 (the full version), make sure that when you convert the ebook, you convert it for "screen" settings because that way it will be backwards compatible with Adobe Acrobat 3.0, 4.0, and 5.0.

You can configure this in the "Conversion Settings" section of the program where it gives you a choice to convert for "ebook", "press, "print" or "screen".

You DO NOT want to convert your document to PDF using the "ebook settings" because it won't work on Adobe Acrobat Reader version 3.0 and you will have angry people emailing you, telling you that they can't open your ebook and that they are getting error messages.

I learned this one the hard way and it cost me about 40 to 50 extra hours of work in one week and a half until I figured that out.

PUBLISHING YOUR EBOOK FOR THE WEB

If you want to test your ebook in Adobe Acrobat Reader Version 3.0 once it has been converted, you can download it for free by going here:

http://www.7DayeBook.com/ar30.html

DAVID: **Okay. That's a really good point.**

Section 12

How to Set Up an "Auto-Pilot" eBook Delivery System

How to Set Up an "Auto-Pilot" eBook Delivery System
SECTION 12

DAVID: Okay, so I've got my ebook.... I've got a strategy for getting traffic, but how do I collect the money? How do I automatically take payment and deliver my ebook without spending thousands of dollars on systems and software and signing my life away to get a merchant account?

JIM: Okay. What you're really asking is, "How do I set up an autopilot system to take the payments, deliver the ebook and follow-up with my customers by virtually one hundred percent remote control?"

DAVID: Yeah, that's exactly what I'm saying. That's what I want to know!

JIM: And what you're also saying is, "How do I do that without getting a mortgage on the house or needing a degree in computer science?"

DAVID: Yeah, that's true, too. This stuff can be intimidating!

JIM: And the way you do that is with just a few simple tools. You're going to need a web site hosting account and a good one's going to cost you about $15 a month.

You're going to need a ClickBank account. ClickBank charges a $49.95 one time fee and then they charge a chunk of each sale ($1 per transaction and 7.5% of the sale), but you have no minimum monthly fees and you're not obligated to any long-term contracts like you are with a traditional merchant account.

DAVID: **Okay.**

JIM: You're also going to need two autoresponders — and you do not want to skimp on these autoresponders by buying "cheap" ones.

I'm going to tell you a little story about skimping on autoresponders — and I hope it scares the heck out of you!

I bought a program (which shall remain nameless) that told me that I could do "unlimited" autoresponders and it only cost $97 to buy the program. I looked at this and said, "Wow, $97 — that's less than the cost of a really good autoresponder. I'll buy this."

Well, I found out that the program wasn't very good and the way I found out about it is that it lost me one thousand people who signed up for my mini-course. And I didn't know which 1,000 and so basically those people were lost forever.

DAVID: **What do you mean it lost them?**

JIM: It lost the names. The !@#$% thing crashed and lost part of the database and the way that I was set up there was no way to recover them.

DAVID: **That stinks! Let me ask you — how much do you think you lost over the course of a year on that list?**

JIM: I would say, conservatively speaking, that it was a $5,000 to $7,000 mistake, based on what people have bought and based on everything else I know about that list.

I would say quite easily it was a mistake of that magnitude because what happened was the autoresponder didn't work, but I didn't realize it wasn't working. So we kept pumping these people across the site, but it wasn't sending out emails on time — or at all in most cases — and people got upset.

The moral of the story is that I was just trying to save a few bucks and it cost me many thousands of dollars.... and I lost a big chunk of my business's most valuable asset — my list! And all because I was trying to save a few buck on the autoresponder.

DAVID: **Ok, so how much should someone spend for a good autoresponder?**

JIM: A good autoresponder is going to cost you about $100 a year.

There are a whole bunch of different ones that have different features such as how many messages you can send in the follow up, or how many broadcast emails you can send without paying extra.

The two biggest players online that I know and trust are:

Get Response
http://www.ebooksecretsexposed.com/getresponse.html

Aweber
http://www.ebooksecretsexposed.com/aweber.html

I have been using Get Response, but I also have my own service that we're getting ready to roll out.

But you're going to spend about $100 and then, depending on how many people you get on the list, it's going to cost you more based on how many messages you want to send versus how many thousands of email addresses you're going to want to send to on a given day.

Get Response starts charging extra after you go above a thousand broadcast email messages a day, though if you hit that many a day in just regular follow-up emails I don't believe they charge anything extra.

So if you want to do a broadcast of more than 1,000 people in a 24 hour period you're going to pay an extra $30 a month.

NOTE: Any time you start sending endorsed mailings to 2,000, 3,000, 9,000+ people, an extra $30 a month isn't going to mean spit. Pay the little bit of extra money to make sure you get a good autoresponder.

Remember we said that the most valuable thing you have, the most valuable asset in your business, is that list of people? Well if you want to save an extra $20 or $30 and risk destroying that list then go ahead and make the same mistake I made.

By the way, you're going to need two of those autoresponders.

One to deliver the product and one to send out your mini-course to the people who don't buy your ebook right away.

On the following pages, I'll outline exactly how you use them…

PURCHASE AUTORESPONDER SETUP

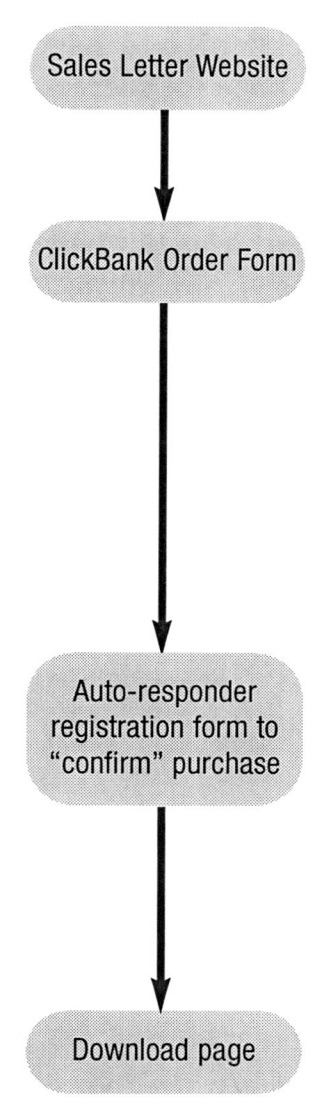

Sales Letter Website

Somebody comes to your sales page and they're going to do one of two things. They're either going to buy or they're going to leave (I'll show you the mini-course autoresponder diagram in a minute).

ClickBank Order Form

From your sales page they go to a ClickBank order form. Once they purchase from the ClickBank order form they go to go to a "thank you" page. What most people do is have the actual download of the product right there on the "thank you" page. The problem is that a lot of your customers won't understand how to download. So they get all messed up and end up emailing you mad because they can't get their product — even though the product was right there for them to download. **So here is the key step**...

Auto-responder registration form to "confirm" purchase

Once they purchase you have them go to a page where they enter their name and email and then click a "button" to confirm their purchase. What you're really doing is collecting the name and immediately sending out an email with answers to all the questions they could ask about downloading, printing, viewing the ebook etc. Look at the BONUS #3 "Magic Autoresponder Message" for the exact wording to use in your autoresponder.

Download page

The last step in the process is to have the "confirmation" page for the autoresponder be the actual download page for the ebook. After they have given you their name and email address, and have clicked on the "confirm" button, then they are sent to this page. After that, once they have received the email from the autoresponder — which should happen almost instantly — they will have (almost) idiot-proof instructions on how to download their ebook.

Both of the autoresponders I recommend will automatically generate the form code for you. All you (or your webmaster) do is put the form on the "thank you" page they go to right after they buy from ClickBank and have the download page be the "confirmation" page for successfully subscribing to the autoresponder.

I had to figure this integration of a simple autoresponder with the ebook purchase process out the hard way, but what this has meant to me is that it has cut down on my tech support emails by 96%.

Figuring out this one step took me from answering as many as 150 emails a day down to answering a dozen.

DAVID: **Wow.**

JIM: Now, you think about answering 150 emails in a day and then all of a sudden cutting that down to a dozen. Think about all that extra time you've just freed up!

DAVID: **Or if you were jobbing that out to somebody else what would that have cost?**

JIM: A lot! Let me show you one of the most important keys that I figured out how to do.

The most important part of the process happens when they go to that "thank you" page right after they give their credit card information and click the link that ClickBank gives them.

Here's what the page looks like when they've made a purchase.

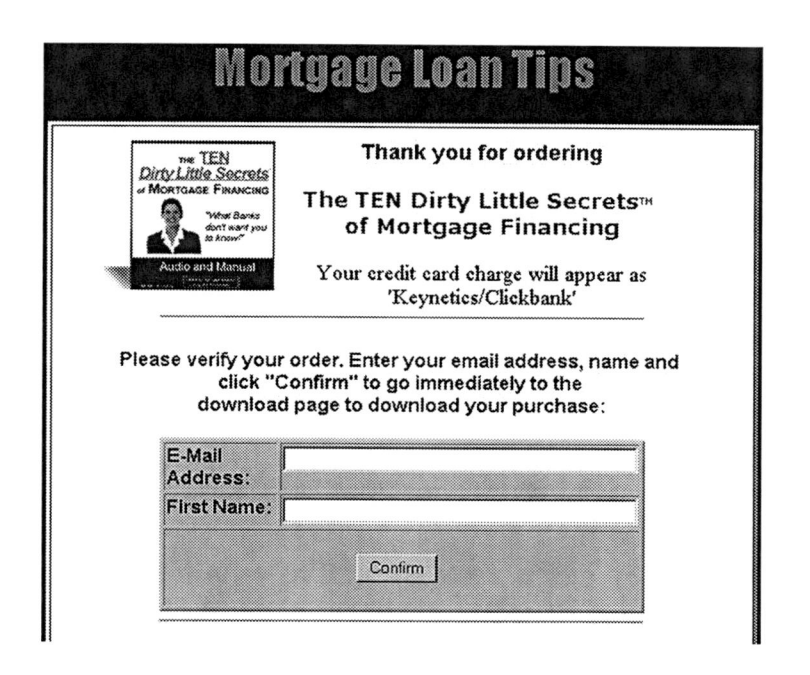

> **Mortgage Loan Tips**
>
> **Thank you for ordering**
>
> **The TEN Dirty Little Secrets™ of Mortgage Financing**
>
> Your credit card charge will appear as 'Keynetics/Clickbank'
>
> Please verify your order. Enter your email address, name and click "Confirm" to go immediately to the download page to download your purchase:
>
> E-Mail Address: [   ]
> First Name: [   ]
>
> [Confirm]

1 It says "Thank You for Ordering [and then the name of the book]" <u>so they know what they just bought</u>.

2 "Your credit card charges will appear as Keynetics / ClickBank" — <u>so they know what their credit card charges will say when they get the bill</u>.

3 Please verify your order. Enter your email address, name and click "Confirm" — <u>tells them exactly what to do</u>.

4 "... to go immediately to the download page to download your purchase:" — <u>they know as soon as they click that button they are going to download</u>. It removes all doubt or confusion as to when they will download.

Now what have I done there?

I have told them what they bought... what their charges are going to say... and that they are about to go to the download page to get the ebook. I've eliminated a bunch of the questions that people ask... which is the name of the game!

The biggest thing I accomplish here is that, no only do I get their name and email into my database automatically, but an email goes out to them that says "Download Instructions and Tech Support" in the email subject line.

They get an email that tells them <u>where to go</u> to download, <u>how to download</u>, <u>how to print</u>, <u>how to open it</u>, <u>what software they need</u> to open it with and all the other major problems that people have that they used to email me for help.

Now they get a very proactive email from me that eliminates most of the emails they would have otherwise sent asking me questions.

DAVID: **How long would it take you to answer each of those emails you used to get?**

JIM: Each email takes between 30 seconds and a minute, and that's when you're copying and pasting the answer that you already have written out. If you don't have the answer written out then you're talking 3 to 10 minutes per email.

DAVID: **Okay, let's say you have the answer written out already. So how much time is saved cutting out even 100 emails per day?**

JIM: 2 to 4 hours a day.

DAVID: **2 to 4 hours? Incredible! You must have just stayed up nights answering all your emails.**

JIM: Yes. I worked from 6:00 in the morning until 12:00 at night.

DAVID: Oh, man. Well, you sort of had to do this if you were going to grow your business, didn't you?

JIM: Yeah. And actually I got the idea for setting up the autoresponder from my dad. And that one thing gave us the idea to write "The Lazy Man's Guide to Online Business" — another very successful ebook I market.

DAVID: Isn't that interesting? Isn't it interesting how it's seemingly little incidents like that happen and you say "Gosh Dad, you know if I could save money, if I could save time here I wonder how else I could save time?" Your dad says, "Well, just so happens son…"

JIM: That's pretty much exactly what happened.

We sat down and outlined all the stuff that they used to do in the insurance business to deal with even a harder, more oppressive workload with no Internet, no email and dealing with it all through the regular mail. Once we laid it all out I then just applied all those principles to my Internet business.

Now let me give you the diagram of how the "mini-course" autoresponder works…

MINI-COURSE AUTORESPONDER SETUP

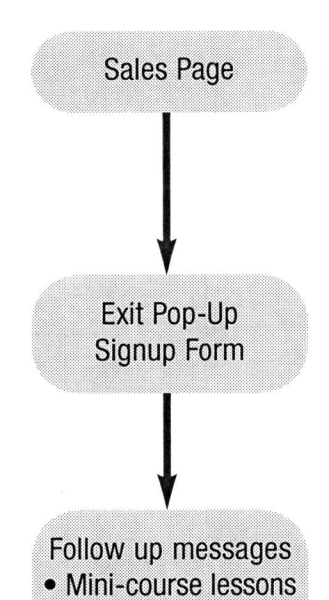

Sales Page
↓
Exit Pop-Up Signup Form
↓
Follow up messages
- Mini-course lessons
- Articles
- Endorsed emails

Somebody shows up to your website and they either buy or they don't. If they don't buy then you still want to capture their name and email address so you can follow up via email and entice them to buy this or other products later.

The way I have found works best is to have the sign-up form for the mini-course as an exit popup window with a very compelling offer of something with a very high perceived value to make them want to sign up. (3 examples below)

You then follow up with a "taste" of the type of content you offer in your ebook that makes them want to get the full ebook and take advantage of what you sell. You can also send endorsed mailings for other, related products to the list.

This is a fast way to build up a list since the majority of people who come to your website won't buy the first time they visit.

Here are 3 examples of exit pop-ups I use that are very effective and have helped me build up lists of thousands of people very, very quickly...

JIM: This is the one we use as the exit pop-up for www.33DaysToOnlineProfits.com. We got about 2,000 sign-ups within the first 5 weeks we put up that pop-up... 2,000 people on your list is a very nice start!

Notice how it has a very eye-catching headline and uses simple bullets to entice the reader to sign up. We also know that case-studies are one of the most popular things people like to get — so we give them to people!

Notice also how we very simply drive people to action to sign up for the free reports by telling them exactly what to do at the bottom of the window.

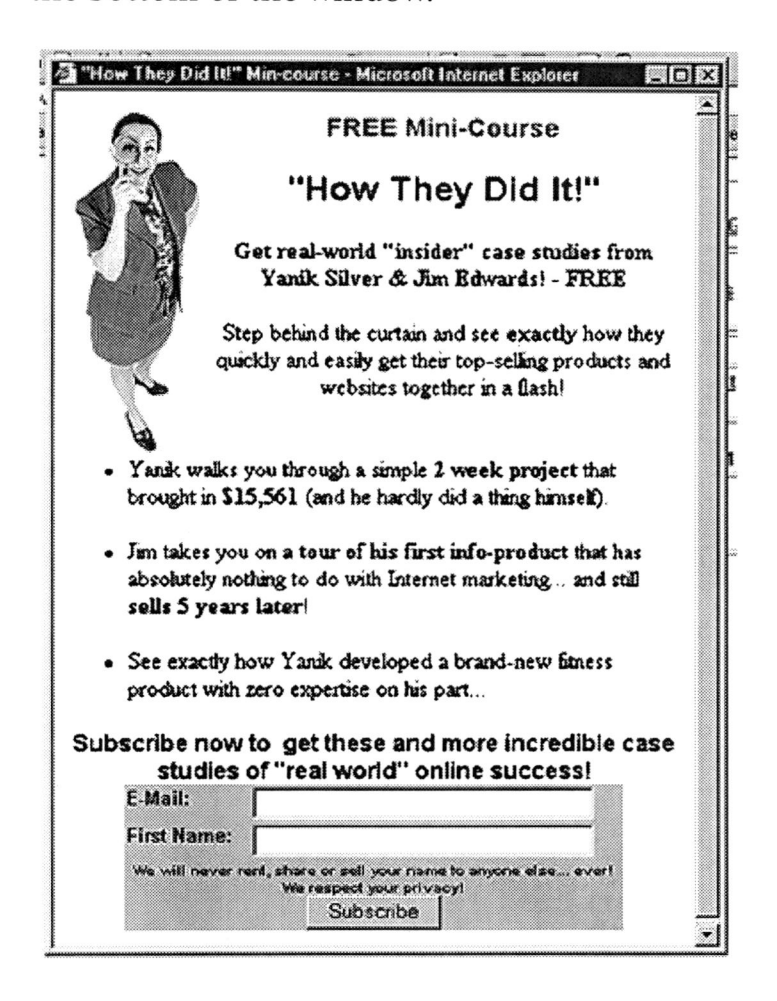

FREE Mini-Course

"How They Did It!"

Get real-world "insider" case studies from Yanik Silver & Jim Edwards! - FREE

Step behind the curtain and see exactly how they quickly and easily get their top-selling products and websites together in a flash!

- Yanik walks you through a simple 2 week project that brought in $15,561 (and he hardly did a thing himself).

- Jim takes you on a tour of his first info-product that has absolutely nothing to do with Internet marketing... and still sells 5 years later!

- See exactly how Yanik developed a brand-new fitness product with zero expertise on his part...

Subscribe now to get these and more incredible case studies of "real world" online success!

E-Mail:
First Name:

We will never rent, share or sell your name to anyone else... ever! We respect your privacy!

[Subscribe]

JIM: Here is the one we use at www.7DayeBook.com to entice people to sign up for our free "mini-course". In this one we tell people what they need to do, but we sell them "how" to do it. Each lesson goes over one of the 4 main parts of writing and marketing ebooks and always makes a strong offer at the end of each message to entice people to go ahead and purchase the ebook.

This mini-course relies almost completely on the headline to grab the reader and pull them in… as opposed to the last pop-up window, which also used bullets to entice the reader.

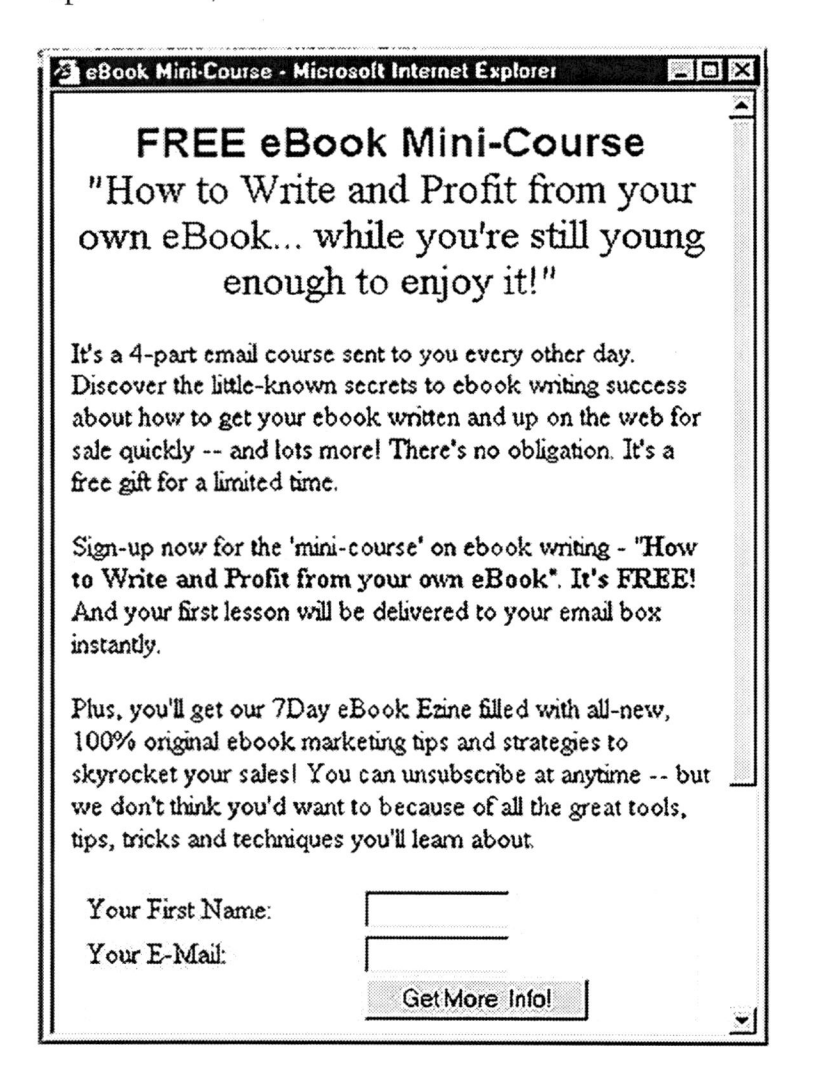

FREE eBook Mini-Course
"How to Write and Profit from your own eBook… while you're still young enough to enjoy it!"

It's a 4-part email course sent to you every other day. Discover the little-known secrets to ebook writing success about how to get your ebook written and up on the web for sale quickly -- and lots more! There's no obligation. It's a free gift for a limited time.

Sign-up now for the 'mini-course' on ebook writing - "How to Write and Profit from your own eBook". It's FREE! And your first lesson will be delivered to your email box instantly.

Plus, you'll get our 7Day eBook Ezine filled with all-new, 100% original ebook marketing tips and strategies to skyrocket your sales! You can unsubscribe at anytime -- but we don't think you'd want to because of all the great tools, tips, tricks and techniques you'll learn about.

Your First Name:
Your E-Mail:

[Get More Info!]

JIM: Finally, here is the one that I use on my real estate book site, www.FSBOHelp.com, that entices people to signup so I can follow up with them on this ebook and my mortgage program as well.

This one makes the appeal of letting people get the first chapter of the book and the table of contents for free... and it works extremely well to get individuals to come back and purchase the book after they get a free sample.

DAVID: **That's fabulous... those are some excellent examples!**

And then is there anything else you need besides a web site hosting account, a ClickBank account and two autoresponders?

BASICS OF A "KILLER" SALES LETTER

JIM: Yeah, you need a "killer" sales letter that converts visitors into sales! You need to have a sales letter that when people show up to it, about two out of every hundred say, "Wow, I've got to have this," and they pull out their credit card and place an order on the spot.

DAVID: **Okay, what are some basics that you need to know for that?**

JIM: Well, the basics that you need to know for that are that you need to either hire somebody to write it for you, or you need to learn the principles of writing a good sales letter yourself. I'm constantly learning new stuff on how to create and produce really good sales letters.

To help you with this we have included as one of the bonuses a pretty good basic training on how to create a down and dirty sales letter for your web site. The BONUS is called "Killer Mini-sites".

DAVID: **Okay.**

JIM: But some of the tips I would give somebody in creating a killer web site or a killer one page web site that's really just nothing more than a sales letter with a order link at the end.

First I would say you need to understand that 80 percent of your sales letter is the headline at the top. So you need to invest 80 percent of your time brainstorming great headlines, looking around at other web sites that are successful, seeing what kind of headlines they have and looking for every kind of way under the sun to adapt those proven headlines to your situation.

DAVID: **Would you care to recommend my ebook for that?**

JIM: Absolutely! <smile>

If you really want to learn how to turn out headlines that make money, then you need to pick up a copy of David's book, "Advertising Headlines That Make You Rich"

http://www.eBookSecretsExposed.com/adheadlines.html

> **Sworn Testimonial by Jim Edwards:**
>
> "I now use this resource at the very beginning of writing every sales letter I do! I literally go through the book and I use the formulas for headlines that David lays out and I just apply them to what I am currently selling!
>
> This is an awesome first step because you would be amazed at the ideas that start flying around in your head as far as all the different ways to entice people to read your sales letter. But if you have a killer headline, the rest of your sales letter can be pretty much average and you'll still have a pretty good closure rate.
>
> Get your copy today!
>
> "Advertising Headlines That Make You Rich"
> http://www.eBookSecretsExposed.com/adheadlines.html

DAVID: **Gosh, thanks. And I know this isn't a copywriting course, but you've done a lot of these web sites and you've had a chance to measure a lot of results.**

So is there anything else that you've noticed that is really important?

JIM: Use a lot of bullets that try to hit your target audience's hot buttons! What ends up happening is somebody buys an ebook because of a bullet, because of one thing they see as they skim through your sales letter.

… and that's another point — hardly anybody is going to read your sales letter all the way through. They're going to skim it!

HOT TIP So that's another reason to use bullets, because as people skim, they are looking for something that is of interest to them. The headline pulls them in, but the bullets sell them!

You've got to include in your bullets all of the reasons that people should buy your ebook. The way you give them the reasons they should buy is by having lot of benefits spelled out in bullet form.

Here are a few of the bullets from the sales letter website for this course:

- A simple change I made to one Website that **quadrupled the sales overnight!**

- How the "**Santa Claus Strategy**" can instantly rack up hundreds and even thousands of **extra sales** for you

- **The very fastest way to make big money** with ebooks — and when it makes sense to use it

- Why you don't even have to write your own ebook to make a **lot** of money **(I'll show you 6 ways to get someone else to write your book for you — for next to nothing!)**

Notice how each bullet focuses on <u>benefits</u> — what the course will do for you, what results you'll get. (Features would focus on the literal content of the course.) The benefits are what sell, <u>not</u> features — but <u>benefits</u>! Burn that into your brain if you want to create sales letters that work well.

This is discussed in depth in **Killer Mini Sites** (BONUS #4) that came with this course.

DAVID: **That's really good.**

JIM: So I would encourage you to go ahead and check out that bonus. They have a pretty interesting looking template that will give you some basic pointers. By the way, one thing I also want to point out is that this Killer Mini Sites package has a real value of $25.95.

If you go over to <u>www.KillerMiniSites.com</u> and look, they are selling this for $25.95. We purchased the resale rights to this — so it's not just some pumped up bonus that we say has this value. If you wanted to go buy this bonus, you'll pay 26 bucks, <u>over half what you paid for this course</u>!

Section 13

How To Keep People From Ripping Off Your eBook

How To Keep People From Ripping Off Your eBook
SECTION 13

DAVID: **Okay, now I've created my ebook, I put a lot of valuable information into it and I know people want it — how do I keep people from ripping it off? How do I keep them from buying it and giving it away to their friends?**

JIM: Okay, let me tell you a little story that happened to me...

I wake up one morning — and by the way, I've never lost the thrill of opening my email in the morning and watching the sales come in ding, ding, ding. That's real money people paid me while I was asleep.

DAVID: **Yeah, it's a nice feeling.**

JIM: So this one morning I started seeing the ding, ding, ding and all of a sudden there's an email from a guy and it says, "Hey, Mike, I got the ebook, let me know how you want me to send it to you. Do you want me to send you the download codes or just email it to you, can I do that?"

Now remember, my name's not Mike — it's Jim!

Anyway, I don't remember the name of the guy who sent the email, or I would tell you. After I read it, I emailed him back and I said, "Hi, So-And-So, I'm a little confused by this email message, are you giving the ebook away to someone who didn't pay for it?"

I knew what he was doing, and I got an email back from him about 15 minutes later with this big long explanation and justification about how he didn't buy it through and an affiliate link and he ought to be able to give it to his friend and I ought to just let him do it because it would save him from having to get his money back and then buy it through his affiliate link and have his friend do the same. He told me I would net out the same amount of money and gave me this big long explanation for why he was ripping me off.

DAVID: **Charming.**

JIM: And you know what?

DAVID: **What?**

JIM: I still had 20 other orders in there of people who bought ebooks from me who probably weren't ripping me off…

DAVID: **Yup…**

JIM: …and so you've got to understand a few things about the reality of selling ebooks any information product for that matter.

If somebody wants to email your book to their buddy, they will;

If somebody wants to give the download link to their buddy, they will;

… but most people won't. Most people are honest.

The thing you've also got to remember is that I can go down to Barnes & Noble right now, walk into the Starbucks that's right in the store, grab myself a latte and then go pick up somebody's book for free off the shelf. While I enjoy my over-priced coffee I can skim through the part I'm interested in, get the information I want, put the book back on the shelf and have exactly what I was interested in — all for the price of a cup of coffee.

DAVID: **Yea… I think a lot of people have done that once or twice.**

JIM: …and so again, even if you've done all the stuff that we talked about, what that means to you is that, sure some people are going to rip you off, some people are going to buy the book and turn around five minutes later and tell you that they made a mistake and that they want their money back and they didn't mean to buy it or they meant to buy something else.

You know that's bull!

Other people are going to buy it and within an hour they are going to email you back and say "This thing sucks, I want my money back!" and you know darn well they are just getting their money back because they wanted to get access to the book and then get their money back…

DAVID: **That's right.**

JIM: …and I still had 20 other people who bought my various ebooks who were honest and will probably buy something again…

DAVID: **Uh-huh.**

JIM: ...and all you do is you just give them their money back, you don't argue with them and you take them out of the autoresponder so that you won't automatically follow up with them and give them the extra free bonuses, and you move on.

If you are really serious about keeping people from ripping you off, then you need to try and use password protection for the page where they download, but the problem is people could just easily email download passwords, and people can easily give their user name and ID to somebody else.

One thing I've seen that actually works, but potentially creates extra work, is what's called a CGI gateway or a PHP gateway. It's a little automated gatekeeper where somebody has to enter their user name and password, but then the program keeps track of how many times that user name and password gets used. It will keep track of what's called the IP number that it gets used from.

If a certain username and password gets used by too many different IP numbers, then the program will shut it down, either permanently or for a 24 hour period. The problem is that, with some of these online services, somebody could just be logging in and out themselves, and every time they log back on they've got a different IP number.

In other words, the program could think the password had been hacked or shared with other users, when in fact it had not.

DAVID: **Yeah, with AOL, that's the case.**

JIM: Exactly, so again you're opening yourself up for potential problems and extra customer support work. However, there are some things you can do even if you find someone ripping you off and they are operating in this, or another, country.

I found a guy stealing my ebook and reselling it — this is just to show you how stupid some people who steal are — but I turned a lemon into lemonade with this. A guy bought one of my ebooks and I was looking through ClickBank at the affiliate sales like I always do and I see a new affiliate I've never seen before. So I click on his link to take a look at his site and I show up to a website that's got my sales letter on it!

He stole my sales letter and was selling my ebook through ClickBank — the idiot bought through his own affiliate link in order to rip me off.

DAVID: **Oh, jeez...**

JIM: So, needless to say, I got hot!

I thought about the situation: the guy is in some eastern European country, so there's no way that I can get the long arm of the law or even an attorney on him. I knew I would have to handle this myself — what could I do?

And I thought, well, in martial arts, one of the things they teach you is to sweep the legs out from underneath your opponent. Don't try and fight him straight on, just kick his legs out from under him and he loses his ability to fight.

DAVID: **Yea, I think in judo that's called "O Soto Gari"...**

JIM: Okay, well, where I come from, it's called "kicking somebody in the kneecaps"!

DAVID: **Alright. <laugh>**

JIM: And so I sent a really nasty letter to ClickBank telling them what he was doing — and they love me at click bank because I make them a lot of money and never give them problems.

I also sent a really nasty letter about this guy to his own hosting company… and I even sent a nasty letter to his domain name registrar.

I then sent a really nasty letter to all of the affiliate links that he had changed in the sales letter. I notified all of the companies giving them his affiliate number and I carbon copied him on every single email… he knew what I was sending out and who I was sending it to — and I was mentioning him by name, website, his physical address and phone number. I got that information from looking up his domain on www.BetterWhoIs.com!

DAVID: You go tiger!

JIM: …and within 20 minutes, he emailed me back apologizing saying he had made a "mistake"…

DAVID: Yeah, I guess he did.

JIM: …and he took the site down. He didn't just make one mistake, he made a whole bunch of mistakes!

So later on that week, after I figured out the way to deal with him, I said, "You know, this would make a really good article to share with my subscribers. I can help them learn from what I did.

So I wrote this article called "Busting Online Copyright Thieves" that has been one of the most widely circulated articles I've ever written! The resource box at the end of that article has brought me business and sales!

Here's the article I wrote from my experience…

==================================

Busting Online Copyright Thieves

- by Jim Edwards

(c) Jim Edwards — All Rights reserved

==================================

How safe is anyone's copyright online?

Well imagine my surprise when I clicked on a website link to discover that someone had not only copied my website to their server — but was selling my ebook and undercutting me in the process! Some dishonest person operating from Eastern Europe had literally stolen my entire business and I discovered it only by sheer luck.

After some very lengthy and threatening emails I got them shut down, but the question remains, how safe is your copyright online and what can you do to protect it?

Traditionally written works have enjoyed copyright protection not only through the rule of law, but also because of the physical difficulty in stealing another person's work. Let's face it, photocopying a 200 page book rates about as much fun as watching paint dry and at 5 cents a page you're talking a quick ten dollar printing bill.

If you steal someone's book, print up a thousand copies and try to get it onto the local bookstore's shelves, the chances of getting caught rank pretty high.

But the online world has changed those rules and physical safeguards significantly. The Internet, email and the Web make it easier than ever to steal someone else's work. With the most basic skills and a few mouse clicks, someone can take your book, your website, and along with it weeks, months, and even years of your hard work.

Though intellectual property and international copyright laws apply to online works, enforcement of those laws is expensive and, in many cases, hard to enforce.

Well don't despair, you do have options if you find someone has violated your copyright online. Anytime I find someone violating my copyright, which isn't very often, I take these three steps in rapid-fire fashion.

First, make 100% sure the other person realizes they have violated your copyright. You can send them a nice but firm note telling them to stop whatever activity violates your copyright. If that doesn't work move on to step two.

Second, once you know with 100% certainty they understand they have violated your copyright, yet refuse to respond or stop, you need to shut them down by eliminating their ability to do business!

Send them an email with a carbon copy sent to their Internet Service Provider (ISP), their credit card processor, their web hosting company, and even the company that sold them their domain name.

Finally, follow this email up with a hard copy letter to each party sent via registered mail. In the email and letter detail exactly how they have blatantly violated your copyright and you want them to desist immediately.

By taking this approach you can often just bypass the offending party because the companies enabling them to transact business don't want any trouble. If you can show copyright violation they will shut the perpetrator down to avoid getting sued themselves.

Though not foolproof, this strategy can help you when facing down a blatant online copyright violator. Just remember to act quickly, thoroughly and don't hesitate to contact your attorney for advice.

Author's Note: By no means let this article dampen your enthusiasm for operating your business or selling your ebook online!

In my opinion there is no better way to make a living!

Your copyright is basically as safe online as it is offline. However, if a sneak thief entered your home — you'd call the cops. Well, now you know what to do if a sneak thief ever gives you trouble online!

You can also get more information about copyright law by going to

http://lcweb.loc.gov/copyright/

================================

Why are some people getting rich selling their ebooks?

> Jim Edwards and Joe Vitale have created the *ultimate* guide -
>
> "How to Write and Publish your own Outrageously Profitable eBook... in as little as 7 Days!"
>
> FREE Details: ==> http://www.7DayeBook.com
>
> =================================
>
> ** Attn Ezine editors / Site owners **
>
> Feel free to reprint this article in its entirety in your ezine or on your site so long as you leave all links in place, do not modify the content and include our resource box as listed above.
>
> Feel free to substitute your affiliate link in place of our link in the resource box.
>
> Earn 50% on every purchaser you refer.
>
> Affiliate details are available here:
>
> http://www.7DayeBook.com/affiliateinfo.shtml
>
> If you do use the material please send us a note so we can take a look. Thanks.

DAVID: **That's great...**

JIM: So because people are really concerned about this issue of copyright, I turned how I dealt with this idiot into a story that people could benefit from and I ended up getting a lot of traffic from my web site as a result.

DAVID: Yeah, and it's a really interesting point, because everyone thinks they are alone on the Internet, but the fact is it is an interdependent community. It's great how one person, without a lot of lawyers and a lot of machinery, just by stating some facts to the right people in the right way, can turn the situation around in 20 minutes....

That's a great story.

Section 14

A Surefire Way to Increase eBook Sales by Helping Your Affiliates Make More Money

A Surefire Way to Increase eBook Sales by Helping Your Affiliates Make More Money

SECTION 14

JIM: You know what, telling that story about the guy ripping me off just made me thing about an awesome technique I use to increase sales without spending a dime on advertising or additional traffic!

DAVID: Well, don't keep it to yourself.

JIM: Alright — here it is, a tip that's worth its weight in gold 100 times over.

When somebody buys from you through ClickBank, on the order management page it will show you which affiliate sold it. Any time you have an affiliate sale, you need to click on that link and go to that affiliate's site, find out who they are and send them an email that says something to the effect of, "Hey thanks a lot for the sale, is there anything I can do to help you make more money?"

I've gotten some guys, gals who just sold one ebook kind of by accident or just testing me out because they found me through the ClickBank Marketplace and could sign up for my affiliate program automatically. I sent them a simple little email like that, they were so impressed that they ended up doing an endorsed mailing to their list about my product and we sold a couple hundred ebooks to their list…

DAVID: **Wow!**

JIM: … all because nobody does that, nobody says "thank you" anymore…

DAVID: **That is, I mean it's not a million dollar idea, but it sure is a ten thousand dollar idea!**

JIM: Nobody says thank you and any time somebody does something…

DAVID: **…and even if they say thank you, nobody says is there anything I can do to help you make more money…**

JIM: … I make sure I thank them for the sales we do get…

DAVID: **…What a great idea… a great idea!**

JIM: I've done that with big time marketers too.

I've said something to the effect of, "You know, my list isn't as big as yours, but is there anything I can do to help you make more money?" And they're shocked that you would ask, "Can I help you?" — they can't help but be genuinely impressed that you would ask sincerely.

In fact, it's called common courtesy, and that will get you pretty far down the road.

I found another guy (who actually found me by accident). This guy found me, I had no idea who he was, and I'm not going to tell you his name…

DAVID: ...Alright...

JIM: ...but he started selling my ebook one night... the sales just appeared (he found me through the ClickBank Market Place or from someone else sending out an email about it).

So I sent the guy the email thanking him, and about ten minutes later, he emails me back and he says, "You're welcome! I don't need any help, but how about a free evaluation copy of the book?"

I looked and saw the guy had sold five ebooks in the last hour and a half and I went, "Heck yes, here you go, is there anything else I can do to help you?"

HOT TIP — He said "No, but I'm glad to see that there's a real person on the other end of this email and I'll see what I can do to sell some more."

This guy sells 30 to 40 ebooks a month for me now... and he's still selling!

DAVID: **And how much money does that put in your pocket?**

JIM: Anywhere between $400 and $600 a month.

DAVID: **That's interesting... and all because you bothered to send him a simple email thanking him for selling your ebook...**

JIM: Right. And, I gave him a free copy of the book.

See, creating those relationships is what you are really after. I now have people who I haven't even known for a year that I can email and say, "Hey, I've got this new product and this is what it does and this why it is great, this is how much money you're going to make and here's some proven copy — would you mind running it?"

The majority of them, unless they have a whole bunch of stuff lined up in their advertising queue, will take it and run with it!

DAVID: **An experienced online marketer would KILL to have contacts like that!**

JIM: Most of those people have come either by accident or by referral. But it's not really by accident because, as you know, luck is just "preparation meeting opportunity" — it's just constantly being aware of what's going on and focusing on how I can benefit them <u>first</u>!

DAVID: **… and responding.**

JIM: Yes. By responding quickly or by being the first one to take action… to take a proactive position and by responding with <u>what is in it for them</u>.

See most people are walking around listening to one radio station and that is WIFM and that stands for, "**W**hat's **I**n **I**t **F**or **M**e". If you can play their favorite song on their favorite station then they'll tune in to you a whole lot more often… and even turn up the volume.

DAVID: **And what's their favorite song? <smile>**

JIM: Let's see, they like to hear "What are you going to do for me?", or the latest hit of, "How can you make me money today?", or that old favorite of, "How can you benefit me today?" <laugh>

You can play all those "songs" for them because it's going to make you money too.

> **HOT TIP:** **STOP** worrying about how **you're** going to make money. Start thinking about **how you can help THEM make money** with your product.

Another place where I like to find people to contact about selling my product is through my website statistics program. You can usually look through your website stats, but that really depends on how your stats are set up and how your web site hosting account is set up.

With ClickBank it's real easy to tell when affiliates are sending you traffic.

The entry in the stats may look something like this:

http://hop.clickbank.net/r.cgi?http:/www.7dayebook.com/?hop=efbook.7dayebook

> **HOT TIP:** In this case "efbook" is the affiliate and 7dayebook is my site. If you want to see who "efbook" is then you can create a little "reverse" link that will show you who they are — if their site is set up with ClickBank — sometimes they aren't set up and this won't work.

Create a link like this:
http://hop.clickbank.net/?[yourID]/[theirID]

So in this case it would be:
http://hop.clickbank.net/?7dayebook/efbook

And you would see that takes you to "The Lazy Man's Guide" — it's a reverse lookup way to see who is sending you traffic through ClickBank.

Your stats may also just give you the URL (web page address) of sites that are sending you traffic. You can just copy and paste those into your web browser and see who is sending the traffic.

A SUREFIRE WAY TO INCREASE EBOOK SALES...

DAVID: **Why do you want to see who is sending you traffic? Why are you going to the trouble?**

JIM: Because I'm looking for the affiliate who is already sending me traffic that isn't making as many sales as he could. I want to reach out to them and see how I can help them generate more sales.

Maybe it's by helping them display the sales message better on their web site -or choose a different headline — or use a graphic — or a text link instead of a graphic. Whatever it takes, I want to help them!

DAVID: **Because these guys and gals are your commission sales force that you are not paying a dime to have working for you 24/7.**

JIM: Exactly, you don't pay a dime to them until they make a sale. And if you're using **ClickBank** you're not even the one cutting the check. ClickBank handles all the bookkeeping and does all the payments for you.

Also, with the ClickBank Marketplace they can automatically sign up as affiliates... so you have to proactively find them and work with them.

Reaching out to affiliates — that's the kind of stuff that makes you money... and it doesn't cost you an extra dime to generate the traffic!

Section 15

"WAR Stories"

"WAR Stories"
SECTION 15

DAVID: **Jim, I know you have a few really good "straight from the front lines" type stories to tell. Can we hear them?**

STORY #1 — HOW A 1 HOUR AND 20 MINUTE PHONE CALL CHANGED MY LIFE!

JIM: In August of this past year, I had a change in job situation and was contemplating my options. I had a conversation with a buddy of mine, Yanik Silver, who I had done some work with, but we had not collaborated with each other on anything. I told him about the job situation when we talked on the phone one night.

We were just kicking around ideas — Yanik knew I had done a project with Joe Vitale, so Yanik told me, "Hey, if you ever want to do a joint venture or something, just let me know."

I said, "Well, you know, let's kick around some ideas" and so I was standing next to my bookcase and we started thinking. We started thinking about what people who we could directly contact were interested in learning how to do and what there was a real need for... just thinking out loud and brainstorming.

We kicked around one idea after another in rapid-fire fashion. We started settling in on one in particular...

"Let's create a step-by-step roadmap for someone who has zero marketing experience on the web. Let's give them a real roadmap, a real blueprint."

People love step-by-step instructions. I have found that to be very true because of surveys I have done. In fact, I talk about that in one of the bonuses you get with this course –"How To Use Simple Surveys to Write Best-Selling eBooks & Info-Products". (Bonus #5).

Anyway, we decided that we were going to come up with some kind of a blueprint, but we knew that we had to have an different angle on it. It seems like everybody and their brother is trying to tell you how to market online and make money — though most of them have never done it!

So I was standing next to my bookcase and I looked and I saw my Anthony Robbins "30 Days to Personal Power" cassette series and it flashed an idea — I said, "Hey, let's call it something like Thirty Days to Internet Power!"

Yanik said "You know, the 30 days doesn't sound scientific. How about an off number like 31 days or 32 days or 33 days?"

… and then it happened! I don't remember which one of us said it first, but somebody said, "How about '33 Days To Online Profits?" and as soon as whoever said it said it we both went, "THAT'S the name!"

So we sat down right there — Yanik was in Maryland and I was in Virginia — and in the middle of my office floor with a pencil and legal pad and we started sketching it out… and we sketched out all 33 days.

We outlined what somebody would need to know — where they would need to know it — we'd mix and match — we'd move this up here — we'd shift this down there — and, in the end, we organized it so that somebody could go from zero to making money in 33 days.

Once we had the days figured out, we simply divided up the book, "You take this day, I'll take that day." We wrote each day separately, which is another really good tip for writing an ebook…

HOT TIP That's an excellent way to write a book is to come up with some kind of a "TOP 10" — or in this case a top 33 — or a step-by-step plan.

But we just divided it up into manageable chunks. Within a couple weeks we had the thing written. I took it and did the final edit to "stitch" it all together and make it sound of one voice. Yanik wrote the sales letter and on October 1, 2001 we rolled it out.

That first weekend, with resale rights and everything else, we made a whole lot of money… and over the last 6 months we have made up into the six figures as far as sales.

DAVID: **Do you care to say how much you made the first month?**

JIM: Well, we made over $42,000.00 the first month!

DAVID: **That's impressive! What can our readers learn from what happened?**

JIM: What you should take away from this story is that <u>a great idea came to us</u> and **we acted on it**. There was some delay in there and we actually held off for a almost a month for delivery of the book because we were getting ready to roll it out and then the 9/11 attacks happened… so we pulled back. We didn't release it for another almost 3 weeks.

DAVID: **You were able to sell it in early October?**

JIM: Yeah, early October.

DAVID: **That was a tough time. Everything was very dicey right then.**

JIM: We had our kick-off right between 9/11 and just a few days before the bombing started in Afghanistan. It was almost magical the synchronicity of when we launched it and how we slid in between those major events with enough breathing room not to distract people.

That whole thing, this whole opportunity, the ebook that I will always credit with helping to turn my financial life around came out of an idea during a phone call that wasn't even intending to have that idea.

So you've always got to be open to the ideas and intuition.

> **HOT TIP**
> That's why I like to do joint venture books so much because it's creating that "third" mind Napoleon Hill talks about in his classic book, "Think and Grow Rich". When two minds come together it always, always creates a better product than a product that you create solely on your own.

DAVID: **I totally agree. Most of the things that I've done have been joint ventures. Of the six information products that I've done, only one have I done by myself, and well, actually it was someone else's idea. So, none really.**

JIM: So that's the story of how 33 Days came about from an hour and 20 minute phone call and went on to produce a major 6 figure success… and it's still selling!

http://www.eBookSecretsExposed.com/33days.html

DAVID: That's great! Do you have other stories?

STORY #2 — HOW I DROPPED 39 PAGES FROM MY WEBSITE AND SALES WENT UP OVER 400% — LITERALLY OVERNIGHT!

JIM: The thing you've got to remember is when I started selling my first ebook back in 1997 everybody was saying that you needed to give away a lot of information. You need to really have a "sticky" site. You need to have all this stuff you give away for free and you build a relationship with people first and then they'll buy from you.

Well everybody figured out that that was a lie or the uttering of stupid business people because all of them went out of business! Giving stuff away for free from your site doesn't get you enough business to stay in business!

So I went to a seminar where there was a guy teaching copy writing. And he teaches a pretty good basic way to create a one page web site that pretty much no moron can mess up... so it was perfect for me. I took what he taught me and <u>I reduced my web site down to a one page sales letter</u> and overnight my sales went up by over 400%!

DAVID: Wow. Do you remember what they were before and what they were afterwards?

JIM: Well sales went from being able to cover my gas and being a few hundred extra bucks a month to being enough to cover my house payment, two car payments and electric bill. And that money made a big difference in my life immediately.

The cool thing and the reason it worked for me is because I already had traffic coming to the site. I already had visitors coming because I knew how to develop traffic and I had learned how to do it… in fact I was in that business of generating traffic for others.

But, you see, nobody had ever really taught me what to do with the people once I got them. But once I understood what to do with the people once I got them to the site by using sales letters and I saw that it worked… then it was pretty much over but the crying.

That story really demonstrates the power of a one-page, sales letter web site.

For anybody who doubts that the one-page web site is the way to go and that learning the skills necessary to create one of those sites or to find somebody who is capable of creating one of those sites, this story should lay to rest any doubt!

Because all the ebooks that I sell — all the ebooks that I have sold and have been a joint venture partner in getting them sold — have all been sold as a result of one page web sites.

DAVID: **That's great.**

JIM: So those are the only types of web sites I put up.

DAVID: **Okay. Story number three?**

STORY #3 — HOW I CAN TURN OUT EBOOKS/ FREE REPORTS AND OTHER LARGE PUBLICATIONS VERY QUICKLY

JIM: There is a technique that I discovered for churning out ebooks (or large chunks of ebooks), stories, free reports, or any type of publication that requires a "conversational" tone.

In my opinion, writing in a style of one-on-one communication, just like you and I are talking, is the best writing style for the web. I say that as somebody who writes a syndicated newspaper column and must write in that "newspaper style" — very fact driven and very conscious of space. It's very rigid.

In fact, it's sometimes hard for me to switch gears back and forth between the two styles, but I discovered a technique for doing that really, really fast and I discovered it out of necessity.

Here's what happened... Joe Vitale and I were working on "How to Write and Publish Your Own eBook... in As Little As 7 Days" and the 7 days that we chose to turn that ebook out were also the week that I was moving into my new house!

DAVID: **Oh man, you really do like challenges, don't you?**

JIM: Things just kind of worked out that way. <grin> Yes, I was moving into my new house and this is a 100% true story.

DAVID: **Go on.**

JIM: So we got my office set up upstairs and I had specific things I had to accomplish. Joe had specific stuff he had to get done. I really had this huge volume of work I had to get done — fast!

HOT TIP

Well, I was down at Staples and I was looking for something and I saw this software program called **IBM Via Voice** "Personal Edition" — it's a voice recognition software package. I had tried a voice recognition software package a few years ago and it didn't work very well. Now there's a big difference between the Gigahertz computer I've got now and the 200 megahertz computer I had then.

It was a $29.00 program and I thought, "If this thing could really work it would really yank my feet out of the fire." And so I bought it, took it home, installed it and I dictated about 80 percent of my portion of that book in a day and a half! The program worked great!

And then I took another couple of days to edit it and then we put it all together and got that book done in less than 7 days of total work.

So that tool is really a "secret weapon" for me.

When it comes to creating content fast; when it comes to getting my thoughts down on paper in a way that I'm not real conscious of how I'm typing or worried about my typing speed; or the ideas are coming faster than I can type, then I just dictate them into the computer. That's really a secret weapon.

DAVID: **Yeah, let me ask you something. Do you have any idea how many words your contribution to that book was?**

JIM: It was about 40,000 words — 32,000 of which I dictated.

DAVID: **32,000 words in a day and a half! That's is impressive. I feel like I'm sitting around the campfire swapping stories... only the stories around this camp fire are making me <u>money</u>! Do you have another story?**

STORY #4 — THE POWER OF PERSONAL REFERRALS ONLINE

JIM: Let me see. OK — this story illustrates the power of personal referrals. I've mentioned it in various parts of this publication and I can't underscore how important this is. You should not pass over this point lightly.

One personal referral made me an extra $3,683 in ebook sales in 2 days just by asking somebody for a referral.

Here's what happened...

I was talking to David Garfinkel — yes, that would be you — and I asked him who he knew that might have a list that would be interested in promoting the 7 Day ebook that I wrote with Joe Vitale. David said what I was really asking was "Can we mail to your list?" — and he was right! It was kind of a sideways way to ask, but that is the way you ask for a referral and a joint venture at the same time!

HOT TIP You ask someone, "Hey, who do you know that's got a list that would be interested in this because I think we could make a lot of money?" And if the person you are asking has got a list, and you ask this way, often they'll say, "I've got a list and I'd like to make some money."

David said, "Well it's not quite right for my group, but I know a guy that's got 40,000 people on his list who's been interested in this subject and you probably ought to meet him."

So David introduced me to a gentleman named Larry Chase who runs a site called Larry Chase's Web Digest for Marketers. Larry's got a list of 40,000 people and he ran an ad for me for my book with Joe and in the space of two days sold 127 copies. That made me a nice extra chunk of change and it made Larry a nice chunk of change — and we've been fast friends ever since.

Larry has run other ads and that relationship has been very profitable... personally and financially... all because of one referral from one person.

In fact, I met David Garfinkel through Joe Vitale and I met Joe Vitale by doing a couple of favors for Joe before he ever even knew who Jim Edwards was.

So that's a very good demonstration of asking for referrals and then being very respectful of those referrals. Don't ever abuse them or neglect them because one referral can be worth thousands of dollars for you.

Over time, those relationships are absolutely priceless!

DAVID: **And you probably have 10 more stories where that came from. Of course we don't have room for it in this book, but you do don't you? You've met a lot of people that way.**

JIM: Yeah. I've met most of the people I do business with that way.

Section 16

My Secret Method For Slashing Your Return Rate

My Secret Method For Slashing Your Return Rate

SECTION 16

DAVID: **All right, now. So tell me about your secret method for cutting down on returns. Is there a secret method?**

JIM: Yes. And this is a very important subject!

Let's talk about returns... refund requests. This is another scary subject that people get all bent out of shape about, just like they do with people stealing or ripping off their ebook.

The fact with returns is that you're going to have about a 5 to 10 percent return rate, even if your ebook's really good. Why? Because you can't please everybody!

People are going to read your sales letter the wrong way and all these different things are going to happen that are going to lead to 5 to 10 percent return rate.

Sometimes the people can't open the book. They can't read the book. Their computer's messed up and they can't download it. It has nothing to do with you and they still return it.

So get over it! Accept it because this will help you act deliberately and promote your ebook forcefully. eBook marketing, like any marketing, is not for thin-skinned people.

HOT TIP There are a couple ways, however, that you can **massively** cut down on returns and I have never really revealed these anywhere else!

The first way may sound a bit obvious. However, if you actually read most people's ebooks, they obviously did not understand this principle!!! I promise if you will put this into your conscious and never let it go you will automatically reduce your return rate! Ready?

#1 — **Provide so much value in your ebook that people are going to want to hang on to it.** They're going to print it off. They're going to make tons of notes on it and, in general, they are going to think that they got one heck of a bargain.

Now some people call that selling "dollars for dimes" while other people call that "value added". Whatever you want to call it, the principle is basically <u>giving people more than their money's worth</u>!

A very wise and wealthy sales manager of mine called it "under-promising and over-delivering". So that's one surefire way to cut down on the returns.

Give them more than they ever thought they were going to get. The fact that other people are out there ripping them off and bilking them by selling these cruddy, flimsy ebooks and then you come along and actually supply a heck of a value, people are going to remember that and they're going to buy from you again.

I know it sounds simple — and it is — but it is basically THE most powerful and IMMEDIATE way you can cut down on returns.

But for those of you who want a more complicated solution — have you ever noticed how people value complicated more than simple — go figure?

Anyway, for those of you who want something totally "New", here's your wish come true!

#2 This is a technique that I really discovered by accident, but it was pretty cool when I figured it out and it works great for cutting your returns down to a bare minimum.

Quite frankly, this technique alone is worth many times the price you paid for this entire course!

HOT TIP

Remember that **autoresponder**, that simple autoresponder we set up on the site to deliver the ebook tech-support instructions? Well all of a sudden, not only have you cut out 96 percent of all the technical support emails, but you also have put your follow-up on total "auto-pilot"!

Well, in case you didn't know this, you can program an autoresponder to send more than one message. In fact, you can specify how many days it will be until each new message is delivered.

What you do is in the first 30 days you have a series of free bonuses that are unadvertised — or they can be advertised — but they <u>are not</u> delivered at the time of purchase.

You have several little bonuses that go out once a week for 4 weeks, which just happens to be about the same period as most people's 30-day guarantee period.

To make this technique even more effective, you get people in the habit of anticipating receiving those bonuses — you really build them up!

In your actual messages you tell them, "Hey, as a special treat, in week one you're going to get this bonus and it's going to teach you _____. In the second week you're going to get this, this, this and this. And in Week 3, Week 4 and so on….." — you just drag it out however long you need to over a period of weeks.

The bonuses don't have to be anything big, they just have to be something good the people are really interested in. You know, a 500 word article that adds on to something that they've already learned. Or an article that somebody else wrote, or a tip, or a web site where they can get a free tool that will help them accomplish something or save time.

<u>Whatever it is it has to be something good</u>!

Then, magically, in the end, they've gotten additional bonuses, additional value, but it's also gone <u>past</u> the return period.

HOT TIP

Then about the 35th day what I always do is have an email that goes out that says, "Hey, a little over a month ago you bought from us (which lets them know it's been over a month) and I wanted to let you know that I've got an opportunity for you to make some money with something that you obviously see a lot of value in."

Then I introduce them to our affiliate programs!

DAVID: **Oh, that's smart.**

JIM: And what that message has done is let them know it's been over a month and they can make money with this book if they like it and recommend it to friends or their website visitors.

I start recruiting them into my affiliate program on total and complete auto-pilot.

DAVID: **That's good. I mean that's really well thought through.**

JIM: I used these techniques to grow my affiliate program from zero to 650 affiliates in 45 days.

DAVID: **Yeah, I'd say that's pretty good.**

JIM: To me, that's really good. I mean, I don't have 100,000 affiliates, but I went from zero to 650 affiliates in 45 days.

DAVID: **Agreed. So, who are these people?**

JIM: These are people who bought my books. These are people that have subscribed to my newsletter.

DAVID: **Are they selling?**

JIM: Yeah, they're selling, but you know the thing you've got to realize with affiliates — affiliates are just like the search engines. They're part of your <u>long term strategy</u> and any big time online marketer that you talk to will tell you that really it's the top 2 percent or the top 5 percent of their affiliates that are making any sales.

In fact, of that 5 percent, the top 5 percent of <u>them</u> are the only ones making any <u>significant</u> sales. But, if you've got a couple thousand people that are making you an extra thousand or two thousand dollars a month, that's cool!

You just grow them. It's all a process of growth that you want to move through — everything you do. If I hadn't figured out how to set up that autoresponder to deliver the ebook download instructions, then I wouldn't have figured out how to set up this little technique for the bonuses.

What makes it even more incredible is if you think about it this way...

These affiliate programs or these follow-up programs that people are charging thousands and thousands of dollars for —

I have shown you how to set up virtually the exact same thing and accept payment and follow-up with your customers automatically for $150.

DAVID: **That really is incredible! The second secret you exposed on slashing returns is definitely a killer tip, and that's worth the price of the book by itself!**

JIM: I just thought of something I'd to recycle or re-purpose content.

HOT TIP

If you're looking for content for those extra, unadvertised bonuses, chances are there are going to be parts of your ebook that didn't make it into the final ebook — you edited them out. You can just spice those rejected sections up a little bit and offer them as BONUS reports.

You can also find other people who have articles that are really good that you can offer as BONUS reports.

Another thing that I <u>REALLY</u> like to do is go to www.Download.com and look for free software that does something cool (related to the ebook I'm selling) and show people how they can get it for free. Sometimes, if it's "freeware" — meaning you can distribute it freely without any restrictions — I'll let people download it right from my site... especially if it's a bonus.

This also works well when I tell people that I obtained some software for them and they can go download for free at my web site for a limited time.

Software has a huge, tremendous perceived value for most people — you'll rarely go wrong offering it as a bonus... especially an unadvertised bonus.

DAVID: **Are there specific examples you wanted to give on using these unadvertised bonuses?**

JIM: Well, a good example is the four bonuses that I offer with "The Lazy Man's Guide To Online Business". They are:

1. A bonus on how to get really clear on what you want. That one was kind of fun because I did it with an acronym called C.L.A.R.I.T.Y. where I used the letters of clarity to explain how to become a "Super Lazy Achiever."

2. The next one is how a lazy person deals with problem customers.

3. The next is how lazy achievers motivate themselves to take action.

4. The fourth one is about never pre-judging an outcome and gives examples of how it can hurt you to do so.

All of these were sections of the book that didn't make the final cut, but work great as bonuses I send out once a week over a period of 4 weeks.

DAVID: **Oh I like that... great example!**

JIM: And what I also do in there that I didn't mention before is a couple more parts of the sequence that we go through in the purchase autoresponder.

Let me lay that out for you right now — because there's something else that cuts down on returns and other little problems that can bite you on the leg down the road.

Here's the sequence I use:

Message 1 (Day #1) The first email that goes out instantly is an email that tells them the URL of where to go to download the book and gives all the technical support stuff so that we know they can get it downloaded to their computer. I discuss this message in detail in the BONUS "My Magic Autoresponder Message".

Message 2 (Day #2) The next day I send a personal thank you note from me thanking them very much for purchasing the ebook and asking if they had any problems. I also tell them that if they did have any problems to email me personally. Well, they're going to email me personally anyway so I tell them "email me personally" — it sounds better... like they're talking to the "boss".

Then the bonuses take over from there as each one is delivered and teases the reader about the next one they'll receive.

NOTE: I don't send the bonuses as attachments to the email. All bonuses are downloaded from the website. The messages I send tell them what the bonus is and how to download it.

Here's an example message adapted from "The Lazy Man's Guide to Online Business" purchase autoresponder…

[[firstname]], your Second "Unadvertised" BONUS

Hi [[firstname]]

Jim Edwards here for www.GetMoreDoneFaster.com with your *second* "Unadvertised" Bonus for purchasing "The Lazy Man's Guide to Online Business"!

Last week we sent you a special unadvertised bonus about "CLARITY" — a Major short-cut to a "Lazy Achiever's" Online Dream Business

This week we give you a "crash course" in how a "Lazy Achiever" turns customer problems and complaints into opportunities for future sales and stronger relationships — and do it in a way that creates the least amount of "back-end" work for you!

Unadvertised Bonus #2:

The "Lazy Man's" Guide to Handling Customer Problems and Complaints

"How respond to your customers to create long-term positive relationships using the lazy man's principles for handling problems — large or small."

Click Here to download your bonus in PDF format

=> [bonus link]

And next week, here's what's in store for you...

We're going to teach you how to "push your own buttons" and get yourself into positive action virtually at the drop of a hat!

If your online business is the car... then this bonus is literally the "turbo-charger" that will get you racing to success as a "Lazy Achiever"!

Look for this gem next week.

Thanks again for your purchase.

Jim & Dallas Edwards

> Co-authors — The Lazy Man's Guide to Online Business
>
> "How to Work Less, Get Paid More and have tons more Fun!"
>
> =================================
>
> Note: This email is never sent unsolicited.
>
> You are receiving this email because you purchased "The Lazy Man's Guide to Online Business" from http://www.GetMoreDoneFaster.com
>
> If you do not wish to receive email from us please follow the simple removal instructions below.

Here's a summary of an actual sequence you could use:

Message 1: (Day #1) — Download instructions / tech support

Message 2: (Day #2) — Thank you note

Message 3: (Day #7) — Bonus Report

Message 4: (Day #14) — Bonus Article somebody else wrote

Message 5: (Day #21) — Bonus Tip on finding a piece of software

Message 6: (Day #28) — Bonus Report that got cut from the ebook

Message 7: (Day #35) — Your affiliate program "announcement"

I want you to think about something for a minute.

HOT TIP: When was the last time somebody who sold you an ebook sent you an email the next day to thank you for purchasing it and asking if you needed anything?

DAVID: **How about never!**

JIM: That's right! And that thank you email helps cut down on returns too, because it gives them a favorable impression of us and, if they have a problem, this is usually when they ask for help and I can take care of it immediately.

Also in that thank-you email I tell them, "Hey, you're going to start getting these bonuses as a way of saying thank you." With the 7-day ebook I tell them in a few days we'll send them a bonus that tells them how to price their ebook… because that's one thing we don't cover in the ebook.

By the way — I did that on purpose because I knew I was going to use that as a bonus.

DAVID: **… and these are in addition to the bonuses that come with the original purchase?**

JIM: That's correct. These are in addition to what comes with the ebook as "instant" bonuses. I'm a big believer in a lot of bonuses and you keep them coming because it gets people in the habit of getting email from you that is value-added. By doing this, when you do finally send them a pitch, an endorsement, or a teaser to check out your next product there's a high "open rate" of your emails.

HOT TIP: Sending them valuable bonuses and value-added content gets them in the habit of <u>anticipating</u> the emails they get from you!

DAVID: **Is there anything else you want to tell us about bonuses?**

JIM: The thing you want to make sure with the bonuses is that

a you're adding tremendous value and

b in order to really make this "keep the returns to a bare minimum formula" work for you is you want to really <u>sell</u> in each message. You want to really sell them on the bonus their getting right now and why they should download it or read it. Then, in the same message and maybe even in the bonus itself, you want to give them a teaser for the bonus that's coming next time.

Make their mouths water with anticipation!

So before even reading the one they've just gotten, you want to make them anticipate the bonus they are going to get next. And before you know it the thirty days are up!

DAVID: **Yes!**

JIM: Even some of the people who would have ripped you off a lot of times won't because they want to get that next information and now the thirty days is gone and they forget about it.

DAVID: **That is such a brilliant strategy. I don't know how many refunds you saved but if you're selling a hundred ebooks a month it could save you hundreds of dollars... even thousands of dollars in returns.**

JIM: Yep!

Section 17

5 Streams of Passive Income

5 Streams of Passive Income
SECTION 17

DAVID: **That's good, that's good. Okay, let's talk about passive income.**

JIM: Basically, "passive income" is what you get when you do something once and you get paid for it over and over.

It's the "Holy Grail" for most multi-level marketers, but hardly ever do any of them reach that point.

The upshot is, "passive income" means income where you make money when you're sleeping, when you're taking a shower, when you're mowing the grass, when you're walking the dog, when you're hanging out, when you're in your pajamas.

No matter where you are or what you're doing, you're making money!

That is what people are drawn to with selling these electronic goods, because once you do what I've shown you with setting up a totally automated delivery system, then your job really becomes to see how many people you can invite into the top of the "sales funnel."

Imagine your website has a big funnel at the top of it. Your job is to fill as many people into that funnel as possible so that 1, 2, 3 or more of every 100 prospects you pile in at the top pop out the bottom as purchasers! You want as many targeted visitors to jump in that funnel as possible… the "sales funnel" is just a fun way to imagine your website with people going in the top and popping out the bottom as sales.

Since you don't have to be there to deliver the ebook, you don't have to be there to deliver the initial technical support email, that means you're making money when you're not sitting in front of your computer... and that's the greatest part about ebooks!

You can create passive income

1. from the actual ebook sales,

2. from the back end sales through the autoresponder,

3. from sales through your affiliate links,

4. from sales through resource boxes in articles you write and distribute online, and, eventually,

5. other people will start including links to your information from their ebooks and their websites — which is the ultimate source of passive income because you've got other people making you money!

DAVID: **Yeah. That's what everybody should be aiming for!**

Conclusion

Where Do You Go From Here?

Conclusion
WHERE DO YOU GO FROM HERE?

DAVID: **Well Jim, let's wrap this up. Can you leave us with some final thoughts?**

JIM: Let me sum up everything we've talked about in this ebook…

Your objective is to first create really good quality, solid ebooks that have a market that can be easily reached. A market that has other people who are already in touch with the target audience… who are already selling to this market.

Your target audience must have people who are very interested in the information that you are capable of providing and are willing to pay for that information.

Once you have a cheap and easy way to reach the market and know the market will pay for information, then you create the ebook using one of the methods we've outlined for you to get that ebook done quickly… or to find somebody who can create it quickly… or some combination of the two.

Then you create a totally automated ebook delivery system that takes the money, delivers the ebook, and follows up with the customers so you can just concentrate on finding different places, people, and joint venture partners to pour targeted people into your website until finally you just reach this "critical mass" where you're not really sure where people are coming from.

People are just sending customers to you and they're making money and you're making money and that's when you really reach the stage of "passive income".

Now, are you going to make thousands of dollars a month in passive income? Not right up front, because you've got to keep feeding people into your website and building streams of income through your autoresponder messages, endorsed mailings, the affiliate links in your ebook and the other ways we've outlined in this ebook.

But the key here, at least for me, is to get about ten of these ebooks that are making me between two and five thousand dollars a month. That's the goal I'm striving for. I'm not there yet, but I am getting there because I'm working every single day with that goal in the front of my mind... and working at it everyday is exactly what you should be doing — if "passive income" is your objective.

I have shown you the road map — I've shown you the real deal!

I haven't held any thing back, everything that I've shown you, everything that I've told you is real and it works.

These are principles and techniques that are going to work for a long, long time — this is not a fad that I have taught you — this is not something that's going to just work today and it will be out a date tomorrow — these are principles that can feed you and feed your family!

These principles, tips and techniques can actually make you a lot of money and build and secure your financial future if you will actually use them!

So do not be fooled by the simplicity of a lot of these ideas, because in the simplicity is the power — the long-term power in the whole wide world of ebooks and info products!

DAVID: **Yes! In conclusion I think it might also be worth noting that you didn't pick these simple ideas at random either, did you.**

Everything we've talked about you've tested and used yourself. And that makes the information all the more valuable. Jim, thank you very much!

JIM: Absolutely! "Don't teach what you don't know and don't lead where you don't go." has always seemed a wise motto for me!

Every single technique we've talked about here is a technique I use every single day.

This is the real world!